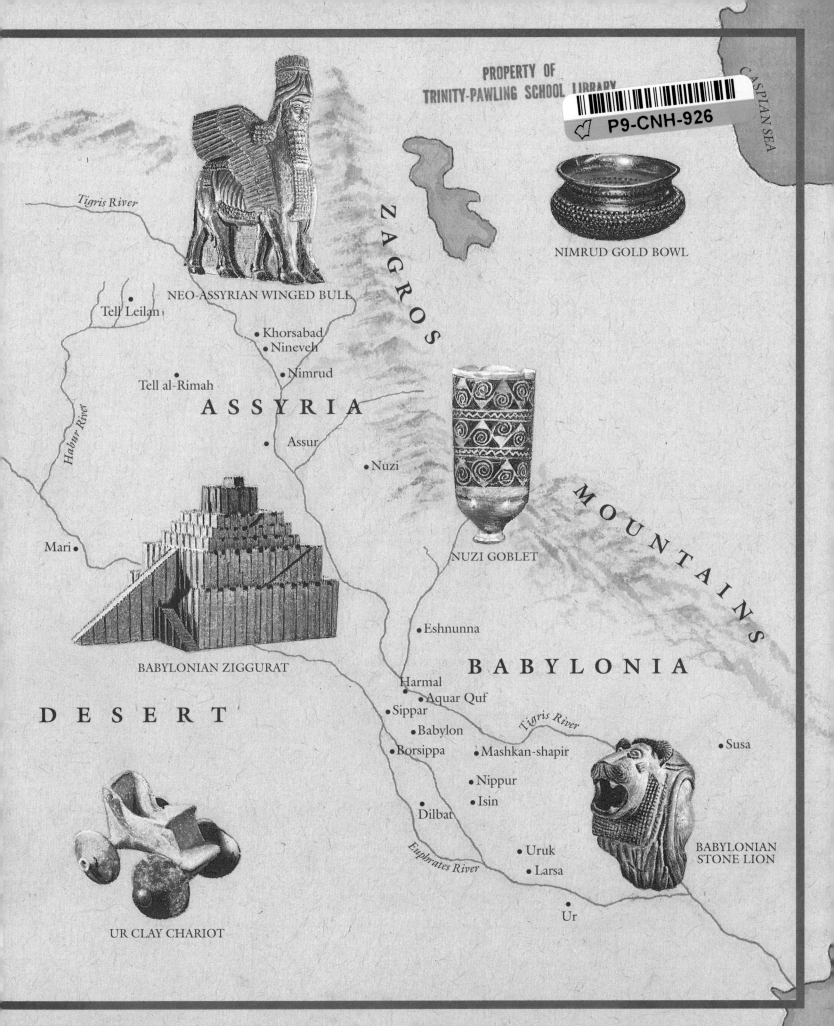

CASPIAN SEA

Tigris River

ZAGROS

NEO-ASSYRIAN WINGED BULL

NIMRUD GOLD BOWL

Tell Leilan

Khorsabad
Nineveh

Nimrud

Tell al-Rimah

ASSYRIA

Habur River

Assur

Nuzi

NUZI GOBLET

M O U N T A I N S

Mari

BABYLONIAN ZIGGURAT

Eshnunna

BABYLONIA

Harmal
Aquar Quf

D E S E R T

Sippar

Babylon
Tigris River

Borsippa

Mashkan-shapir

Susa

Nippur

Isin

Dilbat

Euphrates River

Uruk

Larsa

BABYLONIAN
STONE LION

Ur

UR CLAY CHARIOT

TIME® LIFE BOOKS

Other Publications:

THE NEW HOME REPAIR AND
 IMPROVEMENT
JOURNEY THROUGH THE MIND
 AND BODY
THE WEIGHT WATCHERS® SMART
 CHOICE RECIPE COLLECTION
TRUE CRIME
THE AMERICAN INDIANS
THE ART OF WOODWORKING
ECHOES OF GLORY
THE NEW FACE OF WAR
HOW THINGS WORK
WINGS OF WAR
CREATIVE EVERYDAY COOKING
COLLECTOR'S LIBRARY OF THE
 UNKNOWN
CLASSICS OF WORLD WAR II
TIME-LIFE LIBRARY OF CURIOUS AND
 UNUSUAL FACTS
AMERICAN COUNTRY
VOYAGE THROUGH THE UNIVERSE
THE THIRD REICH
THE TIME-LIFE GARDENER'S GUIDE
MYSTERIES OF THE UNKNOWN
TIME FRAME
FIX IT YOURSELF
FITNESS, HEALTH & NUTRITION
SUCCESSFUL PARENTING
HEALTHY HOME COOKING
UNDERSTANDING COMPUTERS
LIBRARY OF NATIONS
THE ENCHANTED WORLD
THE KODAK LIBRARY OF CREATIVE
 PHOTOGRAPHY
GREAT MEALS IN MINUTES
THE CIVIL WAR
PLANET EARTH
COLLECTOR'S LIBRARY OF THE CIVIL
 WAR
THE EPIC OF FLIGHT
THE GOOD COOK
WORLD WAR II
THE OLD WEST

*For information on and a full description of
any of the Time-Life Books series listed above,
please call 1-800-621-7026 or write:*
Reader Information
Time-Life Customer Service
P.O. Box C-32068
Richmond, Virginia 23261-2068

Cover: His luxuriant beard immaculately groomed, the mighty Assyrian king Ashurnasirpal II—who ruled in the ninth century BC—gazes solemnly from this statue that once graced a shrine at the ancient capital of Nimrud. The statue is shown against the backdrop of a delicately carved stone door sill from a royal palace at Nineveh.

End paper: Painted on grass paper by Paul Breeden, the map shows important archaeological sites of the ancient kingdoms of Babylon in the south and Assyria in the north. Representations of artifacts are shown near the locations where they were discovered. Breeden also painted the images accompanying the timeline on pages 158-159.

MESOPOTAMIA:
THE MIGHTY KINGS

Time-Life Books is a division of TIME LIFE INC.

PRESIDENT and CEO: John M. Fahey Jr.

EDITOR-IN-CHIEF: John L. Papanek

TIME-LIFE BOOKS

MANAGING EDITOR: Roberta Conlan

Director of Design: Michael Hentges
Director of Editorial Operations: Ellen Robling
Director of Photography and Research: John Conrad Weiser
Senior Editors: Russell B. Adams Jr., Dale M. Brown, Janet Cave, Lee Hassig, Robert Somerville, Henry Woodhead
Special Projects Editor: Rita Thievon Mullin
Director of Technology: Eileen Bradley
Library: Louise D. Forstall

PRESIDENT: John D. Hall

Vice President, Director of Marketing: Nancy K. Jones
Vice President, New Product Development: Neil Kagan
Vice President, Book Production: Marjann Caldwell
Production Manager: Marlene Zack
Quality Assurance Manager: James King

Library of Congress Cataloging in Publication Data
Celts: Mesopotamia: the mighty kings / by the editors of Time-Life Books.
    p. cm.— (Lost civilizations)
Includes bibliographical references and index.
    ISBN 0-8094-9041-2
1. Iraq—Antiquities. 2. Excavations (Archaeology)—Iraq. 3. Iraq—Civilization.
I. Time-Life Books. II. Series.
DS69.5.M47 1995
935—dc20   94-24305
                 CIP

LOST CIVILIZATIONS

SERIES EDITOR: Dale M. Brown
Administrative Editor: Philip Brandt George

Editorial staff for *Mesopotamia: The Mighty Kings*
Art Director: Ellen L. Pattisall
Picture Editor: Charlotte Fullerton
Text Editors: Charlotte Anker (principal), Russell B. Adams Jr.
Associate Editors/Research-Writing: Robin Currie, Jacqueline L. Shaffer
Senior Copyeditor: Mary Elizabeth Oelkers-Keegan
Picture Coordinator: Catherine Parrott
Editorial Assistant: Patricia D. Whiteford

Special Contributors: Anthony Allan, Timothy Cooke, Ellen Galford, Donál K. Gordon, Barbara Mallen, David S. Thomson (text); Nancy Blodgett, Anna Gedrich, Ellen Gross, Maureen McHugh, Eugenia S. Scharf, Bonnie Stutski, Elizabeth Thompson (research); Roy Nanovic (index)

Correspondents: Elisabeth Kraemer-Singh (Bonn), Christine Hinze (London), Christina Lieberman (New York), Maria Vincenza Aloisi (Paris), Ann Natanson (Rome). Valuable assistance was also provided by: Angelika Lemmer (Bonn); Nihal Tamraz (Cairo); Marlin Levin (Jerusalem); Martha de la Cal (Lisbon); Judy Aspinall (London); Elizabeth Brown, Daniel Donnelly (New York); Saskia Van de Linde (Netherlands); Ann Wise (Rome), Traudl Lessing (Vienna)

The Consultants:
James A. Armstrong is assistant curator of collections at the Semitic Museum of Harvard University. He has extensive archaeological field experience in the Middle East, having excavated at several sites in Iraq and Jordan. As a Fulbright scholar in Iraq, he directed work at Tell al-Deylam from 1989-1990, when the project was canceled because of the Gulf War.

Elizabeth C. Stone is associate professor of anthropology at SUNY, Stony Brook. She has some 25 years of field experience in Iran, Iraq, and Syria. Using textual and archaeological data, an analysis of satellite images, aerial photographs, and computerized geographic data, she specializes in the overall organization of ancient Mesopotamian civilization and its relationship to the external environment.

Paul E. Zimansky earned a Ph.D. in Near Eastern languages and civilizations at the University of Chicago. An associate professor in the Department of Archaeology of Boston University, he has done extensive fieldwork in the Middle East during the past two decades. Fluent in a number of languages, including French, German, Turkish, Russian, Syrian Arabic, Hittite, and Akkadian, he has taught classes in linguistics and in lost languages, as well as on the Middle East and archaeology.

This volume is one in a series that explores the worlds of the past, using the finds of archaeologists and other scientists to bring ancient peoples and their cultures vividly to life.

Other volumes in the series include:

MESOPOTAMIA: THE MIGHTY KINGS

By the Editors of Time-Life Books

TIME-LIFE BOOKS, ALEXANDRIA, VIRGINIA

CONTENTS

THE RISING SUN OF BABYLON

The face staring out from under a royal headdress, with a carefully curled beard and mustache, is thought to be that of Hammurabi, the great Babylonian king of the second millennium BC. During his reign, Hammurabi brought all of Mesopotamia under his rule.

Down through the centuries, travelers hurried across the bleak deserts of Syria and Iraq little knowing that, only a few yards off the beaten track, cities that had once loomed over a green, fertile landscape now lay buried under blank, enigmatic mounds of earth. To the uninformed eye the skeletons of glittering royal palaces and towering temples would have been barely detectable in the glare of the punishing sun. French archaeologist André Parrot, however, was not such an oblivious passerby. Tramping through these wind-scoured wastes in the 1920s, Parrot heard, as he put it, the "overtones" of humanity's earliest achievements, "an orchestration of mighty names: Hammurabi, Nebuchadnezzar," that evoked for him not only such giants of ancient history but also whole scenes out of the Bible.

In his pursuit of Mesopotamia's venerable past, Parrot lived in "huts made of reeds, which are like ovens at midday and icehouses at midnight," and endured "the vicious and offensive flies; the scorpions which crawl at the foot of the walls and sometimes conceal themselves in one's bed-clothes; the horned vipers lurking in the rubble of the ruins, whose bite would be fatal in a matter of minutes even to the most robust victim." Then on a scorching day in January 1934, on a mound called Tell Hariri in Syria, a dozen miles from the Iraqi border, he gazed down at the small white statue he cradled in his

hands and saw in it affirmation that all the travail had been worthwhile.

Like dozens of similar statues Parrot and his team had recently unearthed, this one had been placed here some 4,500 years earlier as a votive offering to Ishtar, Mesopotamian goddess of the planet Venus and of fertility, love, and war, the last attribute earning her the reverential, if curious, epithet "virile." But unlike the other figures, the sculpture bore an inscription, engraved on its right shoulder in the wedge-shaped script known as cuneiform, which named the subject and associated him with this hitherto unidentified place. The smiling likeness was none other than that of Lamgi-Mari, the Amorite ruler of the powerful kingdom of Mari, rival of Babylon, which in the early second millennium BC had stretched more than 200 miles along the Euphrates. And better yet, from an archaeologist's point of view, Tell Hariri was—as Parrot had already begun to suspect—the site of the kingdom's long-lost capital.

Tell Hariri lies some 250 miles north of the ruins of Babylon in the roughly 93,000 square miles of alluvial plain once known as Mesopotamia, "the land between the rivers," so named for the meandering Tigris and Euphrates, which both defined and watered the area. Yet during the last great centuries of its existence, Mesopotamia was not one land but two, with a flat, arid southland known as Babylonia that differed geographically from the greener, hilly region to the north, called Assyria after its first capital, Assur.

Babylonia proudly claimed descent from Sumer, the southern city-state where urban life took root nearly 6,000 years ago. By

2000 BC a rich and complex lifestyle had been flourishing for over a thousand years in the many compact, densely populated cities of Mesopotamia's southern region. Fed by the plentiful waters of the Tigris and Euphrates, irrigation made Babylonia's fields productive. By contrast, the hilly Assyrian lands of the north were cooler and watered naturally by rainfall. There, cities were huge and sprawling, but more sparsely inhabited than their Babylonian counterparts. Yet the geographical distinctions did not engender gaps in ways of thinking or behaving. Although there were differences in some customs, much of Assyrian culture derived from the older Babylonian realm.

Eventually north and south would compete for power, as this book will show, each in turn holding sway over the entire Mesopotamian area while still other groups intermittently challenged their control. Under Mesopotamia's most ambitious rulers, the empires extended well beyond the land between the rivers—south to the Persian Gulf, north to the Taurus Mountains, east beyond the foothills of the Zagros, and west to the Mediterranean Sea.

Archaeologists divide this dynamic 1,500-year epoch into four periods, called Old Babylonian and Old Assyrian (2000-1600 BC), Middle Assyrian (1600-1000 BC), Neo-Assyrian (1000-605 BC), and Neo-Babylonian (605-539 BC). In the earliest part of this time frame, most of the scholarly focus has been on Babylonia.

An era of great technological advances and cultural achievements, the period was also marked by wars, earthquakes, floods, and fires that periodically destroyed the mud-brick cities. Many were rebuilt and some abandoned for better sites. But in the end, when the last urban centers ceased to be inhabited, the wind, rain, and baking sun transformed them into today's forlorn, eroded mounds, which are known locally as tells and are so numerous that some 6,000 exist in Iraq alone. The tells seemed to some early visitors the fulfillment of the words of the prophet Zephaniah, who had warned that God would "stretch out his hand against the north, and destroy Assyria; and he will make Nineveh a desolation, a dry waste like the desert."

Beyond biblical references and the works of a few classical writers, especially the fifth-century-BC Greek historian Herodotus, little was known of the various peoples who had called Mesopotamia home. Then in the mid 19th century, Western antiquities' hunters began to dig into the concealing dust. What they discovered sparked a long and dramatic archaeological treasure hunt, launched by a procession of colorful characters who followed hunches, made wild but

The Mesopotamian goddess that graces this terra-cotta relief has been identified as Ishtar. Some experts dispute this conclusion, however, saying that the statue's bird feet and wings are inconsistent with other images of the goddess who, in her role as goddess of war, was generally associated with the lion and military hardware.

9

brilliant guesses, and occasionally indulged in dangerous power games in a region that, then as now, was one of the world's political hot spots. But their discoveries, and those of their better-equipped, more scientifically minded 20th-century successors, such as André Parrot, have brought into sharper focus a complex civilization that only now is beginning to be understood. And as the words of the Mesopotamians themselves, set down on clay tablets and stone, are translated in ever increasing numbers, the voices of people silent for thousands of years can be heard once more.

As Parrot and the other members of the French archaeological expedition returned to Mari for a season of work in 1935, a year after unearthing the statuette of Lamgi-Mari, expectations were running high. They could hardly have imagined, however, just how spectacular would be their next finds.

The excitement began with a labyrinth of interconnecting walls, some as high as 15 feet. Gradually, it became obvious to the diggers that the walls must be those of a palace, a structure of enormous proportions—the largest of its time. A "veritable town within a town," as Parrot himself described it, the palace covered more than six acres and included 260 chambers—two of them throne rooms—innumerable corridors, and several courtyards.

Because the palace had been destroyed in a fire and abandoned, parts of it were remarkably well preserved. "It seemed as if life had only just stopped," Parrot observed. Once cleared of debris, terra-cotta bathtubs were found to be ready for use, their drains intact and in no need of repair. Earthenware jars that had held oil, wine, or grain stood in neat rows. There was even charcoal in the cooking ovens. The kitchen was equipped with some 50 well-produced clay vessels in a variety of shapes, sufficient in quantity to set the royal table. The team had no trouble recognizing the king's private apartments. According to Parrot, "They had been placed at one corner of the building, isolated and well protected. Thus the king and his family could live in complete privacy, away from prying eyes."

Dating procedures and inscriptions showed that this architectural wonder was erected by Mari's 18th-century-BC king, Zimrilim, who had enlarged a palace built on the site a few centuries earlier.

As Parrot sifted through the ruins, he came across murals, some damaged by the fire and others in so many fragments that they

Seen in a 1935 photo, excavators unearth a basalt statue of the bearded Ishtup-Ilum, ruler of Mari around 2100 BC, which had fallen down the stairs of the throne room of Zimrilim's palace. Barefoot and hands clasped in a gesture of worship, the five-foot-tall figure is in a devotional pose characteristic of the period. The statue now stands in Syria's Aleppo Museum.

TRACKING DOWN THE ORIGINS OF THE WORLD'S EARLIEST WRITING SYSTEM

The Babylonians and Assyrians were heirs to cuneiform, the world's first known writing system. They doubtless recognized how old cuneiform was, but they could not have known how it evolved. Only today are its origins being understood.

The story begins in the 1850s when researchers, comparing various lengthy inscriptions that contained identical texts in Babylonian and in other, more readily translated languages, decoded the cryptic markings. Having learned to decipher the script, scholars began to ponder its source. Reasonably enough, most would conclude that writing started with pictures that later evolved into abstract characters.

French-American archaeologist Denise Schmandt-Besserat in the 1970s challenged this widely held view. Since then she has marshaled impressive evidence that writing emerged in about 3200 BC—more than 1,000 years before the rise of Babylonia and Assyria. This is when Sumerian revenue officials, who had long used small, fired-clay tokens as counters to keep track of such commodities as sheep, grain, and oil, began to maintain their records by pressing the distinctively shaped tokens into wet clay.

In short order, they were making other markings on their clay tablets as well. The impressed tokens themselves soon yielded to incised symbols that were made at first with pointed sticks and then with the triangle-shaped reeds that would later give cuneiform its name, from the Latin word for wedge.

As shown at right, the initially literal figures gradually evolved into the more abstract cuneiform symbols that enabled Babylonian and Assyrian scribes to leave behind an unparalleled record of their richly complex societies.

Dating from about 3100 BC, only a century after the dawn of writing, this clay tablet is a record of 33 jars of oil and may have been used by a tax collector to tally a shipment. The number is represented by impressed tokens—three teardrop shapes for units of ten and three round marks for units of one—and the oil by an incised drawing of a traditional oil jar.

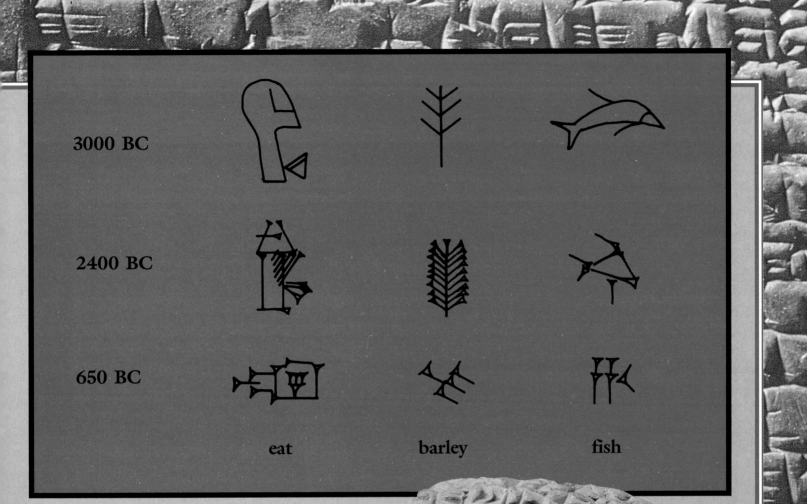

3000 BC			
2400 BC			
650 BC			
	eat	barley	fish

The early pictographic drawings (top row) for such everyday words as eat, barley, and fish were changed over many centuries into formalized signs that could be rendered relatively quickly by a scribe wielding a wedge-tipped stylus.

In this clay tablet from 1900 BC, an irate merchant grumbles that a shipment of copper contained less of the metal than he had bargained for. Shown slightly larger than actual size, the tablet is enclosed in an addressed clay envelope marked with the sender's distinctive seal; such envelopes were frequently used to protect privacy and to prevent tampering with important communications.

had to be pieced together like a jigsaw puzzle. These colorful, still-vivid paintings portrayed the power and significance of Mari's ruler. Yet they must have paled when a citizen seeking an audience actually came into the king's presence. The visitor would have been ushered first through a maze of rooms to the huge inner courtyard. Stepping into the entryway of the audience chamber, he would have seen the central panel of its murals, the Investiture of Zimrilim. The portion that survived shows the king standing before the "virile" goddess Ishtar, who appears in a warlike stance, one foot trampling a lion, with the symbol of her authority, a mace held aloft between two lion heads, rising from each shoulder. The sight of the sovereign consorting with a deity would doubtless have engendered feelings of pride and satisfaction in the power of the king. Next the awed visitor would have entered the grand, cedar-roofed reception hall, vast enough to contain hundreds of officials and ambassadors. At the end of this crowded room, he would have beheld his exalted monarch seated on a throne—as close to being a god as a mortal could be.

While the structures, artifacts, and murals unearthed by Parrot's team at Mari easily give rise to such imaginings, the texts that archaeologists found there provide much hard information about what it was like to live in Mesopotamia during the 18th century BC. More than 20,000 clay tablets lay in the palace archives, so numerous that many still await decipherment. They make a fascinating record of everything from the minutiae of daily existence to the correspondence of kings disputing or commiserating with one another. They include diplomatic dispatches, reports from provincial officials, legal documents and edicts, medical teachings, records of commercial transactions, school primers for the training of scribes, handbooks for the interpretation of omens and the performance of magic rites, retellings of ancient myths and epics, collections of proverbs, and maxims for readers seeking moral guidance. From this wealth of material scholars have gleaned not only facts but also insights into the personalities of both ordinary citizens and powerful individuals.

At the behest of their last king, the ill-fated Zimrilim, the scribes of Mari had kept busy their triangular-headed reed writing instruments, known as styli. Much of his correspondence is official in character, with some documents carrying news from distant corners of the realm, others conveying orders for the construction of canals

In this colorful 18-inch-wide section of a mural from the royal palace of Zimrilim, at Mari, a priest wearing a fringed shawl leads to sacrifice a bull adorned with a crescent pendant tied to its gilded horn tips. The mural was excavated by the French archaeologist André Parrot in 1935 and was carefully restored from the remaining fragments.

and dams. One decrees a census of nomads; another encourages Zimrilim to bring a group of reluctant army draftees in line by having the head of a miscreant lopped off. The royal scribes even kept a strict accounting of the amounts of food brought into the palace, as well as lists of some 2,000 local craftsmen, ranked by name and guild.

Other documents are more personal in tone and offer an inside look at goings-on within the palace walls. In one letter a provincial governor alerts Zimrilim to expect a gift, a wooden cage containing a lion captured on the rooftop of a house. In another the king

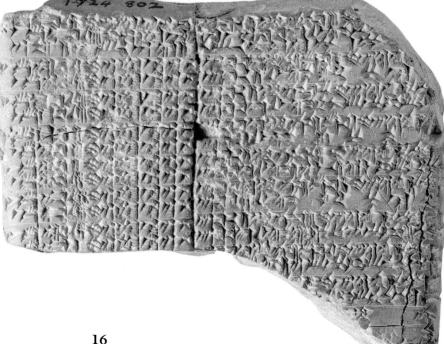

writes to his wife, warning her to take the steps necessary to prevent the spread of an otherwise unspecified "very contagious disease." In doing so, Zimrilim exhibits a thoroughly modern understanding of infection and of the need to isolate the sick person. "Give strict orders," he urges his wife. "No one is to drink from the cup she uses; no one is to sit on the seat she takes; no one is to lie on the bed she uses, lest it infect the many women who are with her." Elsewhere in the royal correspondence, the queen is as solicitous of her husband, sending him warm clothing in preparation for a trip, with a note advising him to bundle up to avoid catching cold.

There are also numerous letters addressed to Zimrilim that tell of dreams and visions and of their portents for the future. Some hint of dark days to come, and indeed, there were already clouds on the horizon. To the south, along a branch of the Euphrates at Babylon, another king, Hammurabi, sixth king in the First Dynasty of his city-state, was raising an army. He was about to thrust his kingdom into the forefront of ancient history.

Mesopotamian civilization was already thousands of years old when Hammurabi came to power. He could thus lay claim to its great heritage. As far back as the fourth millennium BC, the citizens of Sumer, in the southernmost part of Mesopotamia, had made their region

Two fragments of a 3,800-year-old clay tablet show a collection of geometry exercises and questions in Akkadian script that would have confronted young Babylonian scholars. Here students are asked to calculate the areas of various subdivisions of squares, useful knowledge in a society where farmlands were often laid out in long rectangular strips of different sizes.

Based on regular sightings made in the 19th and 18th centuries BC in the city of Kish, this clay cuneiform tablet is a record of the rising and setting of Venus, the so-called Star of Ishtar. These and other astronomical observations were used to predict the future and, as markers of time, are accurate enough for historians to be able to establish the dates of early Babylonian kings of the second millennium.

"the cradle of civilization." They invented cuneiform script and evolved the concept of the city-state, the basic building block of Mesopotamian society.

From the beginning Sumer's greatest challenge was water—enough of it to quench its fields and support agriculture. The region had virtually no rainfall. For society to flourish, irrigation systems had to be developed to tap into the Tigris and Euphrates Rivers, and this effort required cooperation and great organizational skills. Under the creative management of Sumerian engineers and farmers, the challenge was well met, and the region became remarkably productive.

The Sumerians prospered for some 1,500 years, until confronted by the Akkadians, a Semitic-speaking people who occupied the alluvial plain north of Sumer. Around the middle of the 24th century BC, under their remarkable king, Sargon the Great, the Akkadians conquered the city-states of Sumer and absorbed the Sumerians into what would become the world's first major empire. Sargon's dynasty held the imperial reins for a century and a half, after which time his successors let control gradually slip from their hands as his realm devolved into anarchy.

Seizing the opportunity that the chaotic conditions left open to them, the Sumerians enjoyed a brief revival of their own hegemony in the 21st century BC, during the so-called Third Dynasty of Ur, a period when the ancient Sumerian city of Ur exceeded even its former prominence. But destabilizing forces soon were at work. As a prophesy of the day had it, "He of the steppes will enter and chase out the one in the city." And indeed, from the steppes—those nonirrigated lands beyond the cities' agricultural domains—came a seminomadic, Semitic group of shepherds and donkey breeders called the Amorites, who had migrated south from Syria. One archaeologist speculates that they may have been uprooted by a devastating drought.

To the sophisticated city dwellers of the time, the Amorites

This Old Babylonian tablet in the shape of a sheep's liver is divided into sections that are annotated for the use of a diviner. The anatomically detailed model—more accurate than later, medieval European ones—was probably used to teach apprentices how to read the entrails of certain specially slaughtered animals. So important was divination that such omens were taken before the king traveled or his armies went to war.

seemed little more than barbarians, "a ravaging people, with the instincts of a beast," says one inscription found in Ur, and "a people who know not grain," perhaps the ultimate insult in a society dependent on this cultivated staple. A later poem describes the Amorites as being of such uncouth ways that they ate their meat raw, lived without benefit of shelter, and left their dead unburied. But they are also described in the cuneiform records as raiders, a people to fear.

References to the Amorites grow more frequent in the tablets of the Third Dynasty of Ur, an indication of the increasing threat that the Amorites posed to Ur's authority. A letter from the 21st century BC documents the lengths to which the Mesopotamians were willing to go; it describes the construction of a wall known as "the Repeller of the Amorites." This defense, of which no remnants have been found, is believed to have included a system of linked forts and to have extended from the Tigris to the Euphrates northwest of modern Baghdad. Although only textual evidence exists for it, such a wall would have been at least 50 miles long, suggesting that as a human accomplishment it had to have been one of the great unsung wonders of the ancient world.

Not all of the incursions by the Amorites were hostile; it would seem, in fact, that most Amorites moved peacefully into Mesopotamia and embraced a more settled way of life. Scholars have been able to trace their growing influence in the increasing number of Amorite names in texts not only of Ur's Third Dynasty but also of the ensuing era. From the evidence provided by the tablets, it would appear that some Amorites were even beginning to serve as royal officials. In time, the settlers of Amorite origin would adopt the predominant Akkadian language and thus complete their acculturation.

Although the Amorite raids may have contributed initially to the undermining of Ur's dominion, there were other destructive forces at work. According to letters written by Ur's last ruler, Ibbi-Sin, by 2015 BC his authority was being challenged by a rebellious general whom he had appointed to the city of Isin, 82 miles to the south. The king asked this official to send him grain, a request that underlines how interdependent the city-states were at the time, but the general said it was impossible. The willful official then set himself up as an independent ruler.

As the realm fell apart, invaders from Elam, a land named in the Bible and located 150 miles to the east, took advantage of the instability and stormed Ur in 2004 BC. So complete was the city's de-

Found at Dilbat, a modern town near Babylon, this gold necklace was reconstructed from more than 200 pieces and dates from the beginning of the second millennium BC. Its seven pendants represent deities: The crescent moon stands for Sin, the moon god, and the rayed disk for the sun god, Shamash. The two female figurines depict the protective goddess Lama, and the forked lightning represents Adad, the storm god. The two disks with granulated rosettes may symbolize Ishtar.

struction that excavations have revealed evidence of damage in every building of the period. Even more tellingly, a Sumerian poem of the time speaks of the roads and side streets piled high with the dead, of heaps of bodies in places once filled with dancers, of corpses dissolving "like fat left in the sun."

The second millennium BC opened upon a new age, and an inscription on a block of stone found at Isin hints at this next chapter in Mesopotamian history. Known as the Sumerian King List, it is one of a number of such documents, an 1820 BC copy of an earlier list compiled first in Sumer, then updated later at Isin to incorporate Isin's sovereigns into the royal roster and to legitimize their rule. "Ur was defeated," the list notes in the dry, bureaucratic style characteristic of such documents, "and its kingship was carried off to Isin."

With Ur no longer a threat, Isin would vie for power with its other rival, Larsa, 54 miles to the south. The competition went on for about two centuries, a time known as the Isin-Larsa period. Larsa strengthened its grip further with the creation of an Amorite dynasty in 1932 BC and eventually gained the upper hand. No longer the outsiders, Amorites would henceforth be kings and hold other important leadership positions.

Among the Mesopotamian rulers of Amorite descent was Babylon's own Hammurabi, who had come to the throne around 1792 BC and who in time would challenge Larsa's powerful king Rim-Sin for control of the region. By the standards of his tumultuous era, Hammurabi had reigned more or less quietly for nearly 30 years. All the while he had devoted less of the royal energy to warfare than to building temples, defensive walls, and irrigation canals.

Historians know precisely what motivated Hammurabi's turn from pacific to military achievements because the king confided in his close friend and longtime ally, Mari's ruler Zimrilim, through a series of letters found by Parrot at Mari. In 1765 BC, Larsa was still the major power in the region, with Rim-Sin firmly in charge. Hammurabi's letters document how the Elamites attacked the strongly fortified city of Eshnunna, 100 miles northeast of Babylon; as a result, Rim-Sin and Hammurabi negotiated, through an exchange of ambassadors, a defensive alliance. Realistically, perhaps, the Mesopotamians used the same word for both ambassador and spy.

It was not the spying of legates, however, that eventually soured Hammurabi on the defense treaty; rather, it was Rim-Sin's failure to come to his aid when Opis, a Babylonian city on the Tigris, came under attack. Relations between Larsa and Babylon deteriorated further when Rim-Sin sent raiding parties against other Babylonian territories, taking the inhabitants prisoner. The king of Kish, 15 miles away, was warned that Rim-Sin was preparing 270 boats in readiness for a river-borne attack on Kish.

It was time for action. Hammurabi broke off diplomatic relations with Larsa and planned an assault on Mashkan-shapir, Larsa's second major city. Before going to war, Hammurabi turned humbly to his religion for support and prayed to Marduk, Babylon's patron deity, and Shamash, the Mesopotamian sun god. After specially trained priests took the omens by examining the entrails of a sacrificed beast, he felt confident that his army would be divinely led. Perhaps it was this that prompted him to conceive a lenient policy toward his enemy: He would besiege Mashkan-shapir and take the city without destroying it. The tactic paid off, for when the city finally surrendered to Hammurabi, its army joined his to confront Larsa, which gave up after a six-month siege. Hammurabi commemorated his victory over Rim-Sin with a congratulatory inscription declaring that he had "made firm the foundations of Sumer and Akkad."

The king of Babylon may well have seen the need for a united Mesopotamia, powerful enough to withstand another Elamite onslaught. By now a lion had been roused, and Hammurabi vanquished his foes one by one. For his triumphs he depended on the prowess of his heavily armed infantry. Victory steles show foot soldiers wielding axes, others fighting with spears while protecting themselves with metal-studded leather shields, and still others using adzes. Some of the skull-cracking adze heads have turned up, and they weigh as much as two pounds each. For close combat, soldiers carried copper or bronze daggers, or blades strapped to the ends of wooden shafts.

By 1761 BC Hammurabi had turned his well-equipped and well-trained army toward Mari, the domain of his erstwhile friend, Zimrilim. This kingdom fared no better against him than his earlier opponents had, and he nudged its people into obedience under the terms of what the tablets called a "friendly agreement." Inscriptions on clay labels attached to baskets containing cuneiform records and dated to Hammurabi's 32nd year confirm that the city had been occupied by his army and that Zimrilim's archives were being cataloged by the new Babylonian overlords. Mari, however, proved a reluctant vassal, and two years later in 1759 BC, Hammurabi in effect reneged on his agreement and ordered his forces to put Mari and its palace to the torch. The inhabitants fled, and the ruins of their city thus lay undisturbed for centuries.

This two-foot-tall, terra-cotta head of a roaring lion is part of a statue that probably guarded a temple entrance during the Larsa period. Lions—favorite quarry of the region's kings—were common throughout Mesopotamia until the end of the third century BC.

21

Between the 36th and 38th years of his reign Hammurabi toppled major cities of the north, bringing both Assur and Nineveh under Babylonian influence. By the time he laid down his sword in 1755 BC, less than a decade after taking it up, he could claim most of Mesopotamia as his own, having "smote upon the head the totality of his enemies up to the land Subartu," the Akkadian word for Assyria. His victories were accompanied by an upsurge in the prestige of Babylon's patron god, Marduk, who would, in the distant future, supplant the Sumerian Enlil as the chief deity of the realm.

Now, with his glorious conquests behind him, Hammurabi could bask in the Pax Babylonia he had imposed on his enemies and commemorate his triumphs in sculpture. In one inscription, for example, he looked to the heavens for metaphors, dubbing himself "the sun of Babylon, who causes light to go forth over the lands of Sumer and Akkad, the king who has made the four quarters of the world subservient." Once only a petty city-state among many others, Babylon now found itself at the center of an empire—the "gate of god" as its name means in Akkadian. Moreover, even as the tide of its influence ebbed and flowed over the next two millennia, Hammurabi's capital would remain a place of power, coveted by kings, sought by pilgrims, and cursed by prophets as the den of all iniquities.

Hammurabi had little time for further chest thumping in the few years remaining to him before his death around 1750 BC. He was busily proving himself as skilled in the political and diplomatic arena as he had been on the battlefield, and a capable administrator with a genuine interest in the welfare of his subjects. Indeed, if he displayed any shortcoming in his character, it was that he was too reticent to delegate responsibility and too absorbed in the details of empire.

Roughly 150 of his letters found at Larsa and other cities throughout his realm show Hammurabi taking a personal interest in the most mundane matters. One of his officials, Sin-iddinam, for example, was commanded to requisition supplies for the army; to ensure honest compliance, Hammurabi had an auditor sent to check on the numbers of Sin-iddinam's herds of cattle and flocks of sheep, just in case the official had absorbed a few government livestock. On another occasion, Sin-iddinam attempted to recruit men into the army, which prompted general resistance among the draftees. Again Hammurabi intervened, forbidding the conscription of the recalcitrants.

METICULOUSLY EXECUTED DEVICES
FOR DISPLAYING ONE'S IDENTITY

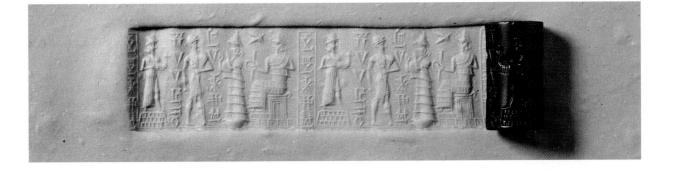

When modern governments authenticate passports by stamping them with an official seal or notaries affix their seals to certify a signature, they are carrying on a practice that began in Mesopotamia some 7,000 years ago. Today, the cylinder seals of Mesopotamia rank among the most intriguing—and often, the most beautiful—artifacts of the period.

The first seals—usually little more than pebbles incised with simple markings—served to imprint on a lump of clay an insignia identifying the owner of goods to which the clay was secured. In time, these implements became more sophisticated until finally, around 3500 or 3400 BC, cylinder seals appeared. For the next 3,000 years, such seals would serve to mark goods and authenticate documents written in cuneiform on clay.

Varying in size but usually small, cylinder seals were carved out in intaglio designs that, when rolled over wet clay, would leave behind a continuous friezelike impression such as the one in actual size above. By about 3000 BC, the cylinders featured a hole drilled through them lengthwise so that owners could pin the seals to their garments and perhaps carry them on a string around their necks or wrists.

Most cylinder seals were made of various types of precious and semiprecious stone, although wood, metal, glass, ivory, bone, baked clay, and other materials were also used. Early seals bore quite elaborate designs; then a period of simplicity set in, before a resurgence of the craft led to a variety of complex and strikingly lifelike scenes. The designs were formed by drilling small holes that were then connected and carved into finished form, as shown on the following pages.

Leonard Gorelick and A. John Gwinnett, professors of orthodontics and oral biology, respectively, at the State University of New York, Stony Brook, have conducted extensive studies to determine the types of tools used by ancient seal carvers. By examining existing seals under a scanning electron microscope, they discovered distinctive tool marks. After duplicating these marks using copies of the drills, they established that softer materials such as limestone had probably been worked with simple chipped-stone drills, while copper drills—a later innovation—enabled the use of harder stone.

One abiding mystery of the seals is how such tiny, intricate designs could have been executed without benefit of magnification. Gorelick and Gwinnett have answered that question by positing that the seal carvers were nearsighted, a condition that is passed on genetically—just as the craft of seal making was likely to have been handed down from father to son.

Crowned with a horned headdress, the sun god stands between two other figures in this enlarged impression from an unfinished Babylonian cylinder seal (left); the lumpy, incomplete figure to the right was formed with a pattern of drilled holes but never fleshed out with an engraving tool. Shown below are scanning electron micrograph views of silicone impressions of the characteristically different drill holes made in ancient seals by a stone drill (below, left) and a copper drill, used to carve harder materials.

Employing the same technique as Mesopotamian seal carvers, an Egyptian craftsman wields a bow drill to bore holes through stone beads. With its string wrapped around the drill shafts, the bow was drawn rapidly back and forth to produce cutting speeds far exceeding those achieved by the earlier method of rotating a drill between the palms of the hands.

A four-winged, fleece-garbed supernatural being subdues a trio of birds, possibly evil spirits, in this impression from a Babylonian seal of the first millennium BC. Made of red chalcedony, the seal bears an inscription asking that the owner be blessed; oddly, the seal maker neglected to carve the cuneiform characters in reverse to make them readable when the cylinder is rolled—they thus appear reversed on the impression.

Carved in the eighth century BC, the blue chalcedony seal at left depicts a ritual scene; above, a green limestone seal of four centuries earlier is carved with tableaus of cattle and oxen returning to their shelter. The gold-capped seal at right, crafted of rock crystal in the third millennium BC, shows a naked hero grappling with a rampant water buffalo.

Three rampant goats appear to rise from a bowl carried by a pair of deities in this nine-inch-tall bronze cup or vase stand. Beaten gold foil covers the heads and beards of the goats, sacrificial animals to the ancient Mesopotamians, and tarnished silver foil covers the faces of the two gods.

Another instance of his solicitousness may be seen in letters to his agent Shamash-Khazir, whom he often reprimanded on behalf of individuals who had complained directly to Hammurabi about the official's actions. The king repeatedly ordered Shamash-Khazir to satisfy their grievances in letters that contain such instructions as, "Content him immediately," and "Let him not come back here and appear before me again."

Understandably, many of the officials around Hammurabi basked in the power and privileges their rank bestowed. Such status extended to their relatives as well: The pride taken in belonging to a well-connected family is displayed in a petulant letter, written by the son of a high government official to his mother, which allows today's readers to eavesdrop on a domestic spat. In the awkward script of a schoolboy, the youngster voices his dissatisfaction with his wardrobe and his annoyance with his mother, both for not allowing him to keep up with the fashions of the time and for not outfitting him in a style appropriate to the son of one of Hammurabi's minions. The letter ends with a complaint that will ring familiar with many a parent some 3,800 years later: "You, you do not love me!"

Among the most important inscriptions of Hammurabi's time is an eight-foot-high basalt stele *(page 29)*, now in the Louvre. It is engraved with the famous Code of Hammurabi, and some scholars believe it once stood in the temple of Marduk in Babylon. Seized as booty by the Elamites in the 12th century BC, it was carried off to their capital at Susa in present-day Iran, where the monument was discovered in 1901 by French archaeologists. Part of the inscription was erased, presumably by the Elamites, although scholars have since been able to restore the missing text using fragments of a second, similarly worded stele, as well as copies of the laws written on clay tablets and stored in the library of the seventh-century-BC Assyrian king Ashurbanipal, 240 miles north of Babylon at Nineveh.

The code consists of 282 laws bracketed at the beginning and end by a prologue and epilogue. Touching upon almost every aspect of everyday life in Babylonia, the laws were allegedly written, as the prologue states, "to cause justice to prevail in the land, to destroy the wicked and the evil, that the strong may not oppress the weak." Each law took the form of a conditional sentence: If someone committed this act, then the offending party could expect that punishment. Moreover, many of the injunctions were of the eye-for-an-eye variety, with death prescribed for murderers and broken bones for those who broke the bones of others. Amputation was demanded for any surgeon whose malpractice resulted in a patient's death, unless the deceased happened to have been a slave, in which case the physician only had to make good on the master's lost property.

Three social classes are delineated in the code. The freeman or full-fledged citizen was held in the highest regard. Next in rank was the second-class individual, who may even have been a ward of the state. And at the bottom of the ladder was the slave. Class mattered greatly when penalties were meted out. For a freeman who had struck another freeman, for example, the suggested fine was one mina, or an 18-ounce bar of silver. An individual of the second class who walloped his peer paid a smaller fine, 10 shekels of silver, or about one-sixth of the freeman's penalty. Not surprisingly, the slave got the shortest shrift, for while one slave could conceivably hit another with impunity, the slave who smacked a freeman had his ear lopped off.

A slave would have been easily recognized by his *abbuttum*, a distinctive lock of hair. Fear of runaway slaves must have been great, for woe to the barber who dared to trim off an abbuttum without the master's consent. Hammurabi's code called for the amputation of the barber's hand. A man who forced a barber to shave the abbuttum of another man's slave faced a truly stiff penalty—death and impalement in his own doorway. The barber had only to take an oath that he was an unwitting participant to earn his release.

Other punishments were no less exacting. For example, a contractor whose slapdash work led to the collapse of a home and the death of the owner could expect to be put to death himself; a woman who neglected her house and humiliated her husband would be forced to undergo trial by water, with the nearest river as judge—the verdict entirely dependent on her ability to swim. With such strict punishments, accusations of wrongdoing were not made lightly. A man who falsely accused the wife of another man of a crime would be dragged before the judges himself and summarily relieved of half his hair.

Laws relating to family matters abound in the code. Adoption, for example, was recognized and protected. If a citizen adopted and reared a child, the youth could never be reclaimed; but if the adoptive father himself sought out the youngster's parents, then the child could be returned to his original home.

Several of these statutes suggest that a motivation for turning children over to foster families might have been to improve a youngster's economic chances by enabling the child to learn a trade. If an artisan adopted a boy and taught him his handicraft, the youth could not be reclaimed; but if the craftsman failed to pass on his skills, then the youngster could return to his parental abode.

Sexual abusers of women and children were punished severely when incest was the issue. A man who slept with his daughter faced exile; if the abuse occurred with his son's wife, the man was bound and thrown into the river and left to drown. The punishment was even worse if the man had sex with his own mother: Both parties were burned to death.

Archaeologists have been struck by the similarity of the Code of Hammurabi to the laws of Moses. Both express concern, for example, for the helpless, such as widows and orphans, and both attempt to prescribe punishment that is appropriate to the crime but not excessive. Scholars have suggested that each set of laws had its roots in a common tradition.

Hammurabi's statutes drew on a longstanding legal tradition that can be traced back to a code of the Isin-Larsa period immediately preceding Hammurabi's, known as the laws of Eshnunna, and even further back to the Sumerian laws of Ur-Nammu, founder of the Third Dynasty of Ur, around 2100 BC. Written on tablets unearthed at Ur and in the ruins of Nippur, a major city 54 miles southeast of Babylon, Ur-Nammu's code, like Hammurabi's, sought to prescribe retribution precisely suited to the crime, with the punishment usually meted out in the form of fines. One of Hammurabi's laws—"If someone severed the nose of another man with a copper knife, he must pay two-thirds of a mina of silver"—is echoed in a similarly worded law of Eshnunna. The last, however, had an additional clause—for biting off someone's nose, the fine was a full mina of silver. The even stricter "eye-for-an-eye, tooth-for-a-tooth" concept is believed to have been a Hammurabi innovation, perhaps inspired by Amorite traditions.

Despite Hammurabi's own plea that future kings "give heed to the words which I have inscribed on my stele," his heirs appear to

The capital of the stele inscribed with the Code of Hammurabi shows the king in prayer before the highest of all judges, the enthroned Shamash. Despite his apparent humility before the god, Hammurabi, in the prologue to his 49 columns of law, declares himself "god among kings," "a fighter without peer," and "the one who plumbed the depths of wisdom."

have largely ignored both his will and his laws. Of the thousands of legal documents that date from the Old Babylonian period, only one—a contract found at Ur—uses Hammurabi's code as a legal precedent and, even then, only in a single penalty clause.

For all the greatness of the man, little survives of Hammurabi's Babylon because a new city, the Babylon of Nebuchadnezzar II, conqueror of Jerusalem, was built atop the waterlogged ruins of the old in the sixth century BC, 12 centuries after Hammurabi's death. But the dry and therefore more accessible ruins of other, more complete, urban centers of his day, including Ur (which had been rebuilt after its destruction by the Elamites), Nippur, and Mashkan-shapir, an important trade town, suggest what his Babylon must have been like.

In Ur the private houses lining the streets date from the time when the city came under the thumb first of Larsa, then of Hammurabi. The houses were destroyed around 1740 BC by Hammurabi's son, Samsuiluna. As at Mari, the deliberately set fires that ravaged Ur turned the mud-brick city—and its clay-tablet documents—into a kind of time capsule. Indeed, from the well-preserved remains Ur's excavator, British archaeologist Sir Leonard Woolley, was even able to identify owners of individual dwellings and shops.

Families occupied either one-story houses, as many archaeologists believe today, or two-story homes, as Woolley thought, made of plastered, whitewashed brick. No windows faced the narrow, winding streets on the first floor. Typically a house rose around a central courtyard, yet no two homes were alike, due to the need to build on irregularly shaped lots of various sizes. In one, the second floor or roof was reached by a doorway leading to steps constructed over the bathroom, a narrow room with a paved floor containing a hole for the drain. Woolley surmised that the ground floor was presumably where visitors were received and servants slept; the family's private quarters apparently lay upstairs. Even if the houses were only one story, it is thought that families slept on their roofs for most of the year, when the weather was warm enough.

The roof of such a house, sloping very gently toward the courtyard, had gutters placed at intervals, directing rainfall toward a drain in the middle of the brick-paved floor, which inclined toward the outlet. Such a house, wrote Woolley, "implies a standard of life of a really high order. And these are the houses not of particularly wealthy people but, as the tablets found in them prove, of the middle class—shopkeepers, petty merchants, scribes, and so on whose fortunes and idiosyncracies we can sometimes trace quite vividly."

In one of Ur's houses, that of a schoolmaster named Igmil-Sin, Woolley came upon hundreds of bun-shaped clay tablets that had been used by the teacher's students to practice their cuneiform. Excavations carried out at Nippur in the early 1950s by two archaeologists from the Oriental Institute at the University of Chicago, Donald McCown and Richard Haines, revealed another house that also served as a school. There were two classrooms, one inside, presumably used during cold weather, with benches around the walls where students sat, and the other outdoors in the courtyard, as evidenced by the presence of similar seats. Here a large pot was found with many little vessels inside it. The students presumably dipped water from the pot into the small jars and used the contents to keep their clay tablets moist while writing on them.

At Ur Woolley uncovered documents stored in pots in the main living rooms of houses. These were the kinds of records that today might be kept in safe-deposit boxes: contracts detailing the purchase and sale of houses, land, and slaves; wills, loans, marriage and adoption records; and the proceedings of cases that had been taken to court—a wealth of intriguing information about everyday life.

Similar documents have been found stored in private homes in other cities. One text was a transcription of a trial in Nippur, in a neighborhood court that judged domestic cases. The testimony ex-

A SEARCH FOR THE ELUSIVE
BIBLICAL PATRIARCH ABRAHAM

Did Abraham, the patriarch revered by Christians, Jews, and Muslims alike, really exist? According to the Old Testament, Abraham moved with his father from "Ur of the Chaldees"—Chaldea being the biblical name for Mesopotamia—to Harran, on the area's northwestern frontier. There, so Jewish legend has it, he turned against the religion of his father, a maker of idols, shattering the graven images, then left with wife and retinue for the Promised Land, as depicted in this 16th-century painting.

Abraham has been deemed by many influential scholars to be a mythical character meant to personify traditional events of early biblical times, while others have insisted that he was a historical figure. W. F. Albright, an American archaeologist, sifted through archaeological and written data in an attempt to uncover the historical Abraham by establishing a time period for the milieu described in Genesis. He concluded that Abraham had lived sometime around 1800 BC.

During excavations at Tell al-Muqayyar in southern Iraq between 1922 and 1934, British archaeologist Leonard Woolley discovered structures from the early part of the second millennium and, following Albright's dating, suggested to the world,

in his popular works at least, that this site might be Abraham's city, Ur of the Chaldees. Among the jumbled ruins, Woolley unearthed foundations of numerous substantial houses, any one of which, he suggested, might have been Abraham's boyhood home. His suppositions were eagerly accepted by the public and many biblical historians.

But some scholars steadfastly disagreed. For one thing, they noted, the Old Testament's Abraham was clearly a nomadic, tent-dwelling herdsman, not the product of a sophisticated me-

tropolis. Moreover, the Bible speaks of Abraham's traveling with a caravan of camels, but the camel was not widely domesticated until centuries after the time frame suggested by Albright and Woolley. In addition, scholars like American Thomas L. Thomson argue that the Bible, with its roots deep in oral history and legend, is unreliable for resolving historical issues. Thus the debate goes on. Not only do scholars disagree about where and when Abraham lived, but others continue to wonder whether he ever lived at all.

posed the relationship of Ama-Sukkal, a wealthy heiress, and her husband, Enlil-Izzu. Proceedings opened with the mace of the city god Ninurta being ceremonially placed before the court. Women then arrived to testify. The judges did not find Ama-Sukkal guilty for being, as Enlil-Izzu had charged, insolent to her husband. Instead Enlil-Izzu was convicted for allowing his spouse to remain a virgin and for pressuring her to release him from the marriage. Of course Enlil-Izzu could have divorced his wife, but if he had succeeded in goading her into divorcing him, he would have been able to keep most of her dowry. Enlil-Izzu, however, preferred prison to life with his allegedly nagging spouse: "I still will not live with her as a husband," he declared. "You can put me in jail until I manage to pay back the money." The "money" in question was from the wealth she had brought into the marriage.

With its flat-lying mane and a hole bored through the muzzle to hold the reins, this 4,300-year-old figurine is the earliest known sculpture of a domesticated horse. The clay model, less than half a foot in length, was uncovered in 1992 at a site along the Euphrates River, some 200 miles northeast of Damascus.

At Mashkan-shapir, archaeologists developed a different kind of perspective on a prominent urban settlement. In its earliest days, around 2000 BC, the city was little more than a "Mesopotamian cow-town," in the words of Elizabeth Stone and Paul Zimansky, the archaeologists who have conducted excavations there. Yet Mashkan-shapir grew quickly to become, in the 19th and 18th centuries BC, an important commercial center where the goods of the resource-rich north could be swapped for the agricultural products of the south.

At the height of its development Mashkan-shapir was about the size of Ur, and like many Mesopotamian cities it was divided into various sectors by a network of canals fed by the Tigris River. These areas contained the religious, administrative, residential, commercial, and artisan quarters. Avenues and bridges spanning the canals connected the sectors to one another. The channels, and the harbors they often incorporated, also linked the city to the outside world.

Stone and Zimansky's preliminary excavations revealed that Mashkan-shapir had been surrounded by a defensive wall, built, according to a text of the period, in the middle of the 19th century BC during the short reign of the Larsa king Sin-iddinam. Clay cylinders—about four inches in diameter, six inches in height, and shaped like modern barrels—found near the city gates attest to the king's role in the wall's construction and indicate that the rampart was raised at the behest of Nergal, god of plagues and of attacking armies, "to increase the dwellings" of Mashkan-shapir by enclosing new land that, thanks to the wall, could now be adequately protected.

At Mashkan-shapir archaeologists walked the entire area, picking up artifacts lying exposed on the surface to catalog and date. This process was supplemented by photos taken with a camera suspended from a kite, its lens of sufficient resolution to discern items as small as a brick. Using such painstaking methods, the archaeologists were able to cover an area much larger than more-restrictive digging would have allowed. From the data gathered, they created a profile of the site—a map of Mashkan-shapir's visible features, including the locations of all the artifacts turned up in the ground survey. The distribution of objects, especially cylinder seals and stone bowls often associated with wealthy Babylonians, indicated that within each residential neighborhood the well-to-do lived alongside the less fortunate, a pattern true of other Mesopotamian cities as well.

Among the more curious relics unearthed at Mashkan-shapir are two-wheel, terra-cotta model chariots, about two inches wide and four to ten inches high. All feature high frontal shields adorned with the figure or symbols of one of two deities, the sun god Shamash and Nergal, god of death and a patron of the city. Most of the chariots were found in the town's administrative or religious sectors, and consequently their use in some sort of ritual seems likely.

While these chariots were not accompanied by clay horses, a well-modeled horse was unearthed in Syria in 1992, together with several sculpted chariots similar to Mashkan-shapir's. The five-inch-long figurine dates to about 2300 BC, making it the oldest statue of a domesticated equine discovered so far and offering proof that the horse may have played a role in Mesopotamian history earlier than 2000 BC, the date previously assigned by scholars. In providing the power to pull fast, light chariots, the horse would ultimately help revolutionize warfare and facilitate the rise of empires. But the advantage of hitching up the animal for such a purpose apparently was not evident to all: A letter from the provincial governor of the nearby town of Terqa to Zimrilim of Mari as late as the 18th century BC advises the king to "give dignity to his kingship" by foregoing horses in favor of the socially acceptable chariot and mules.

Mashkan-shapir was abandoned under mysterious circumstances, perhaps as part of the same crisis that led to the desertion of cities in central and southern Babylonia around 1720 BC, during the reign of Hammurabi's successor, his son Samsuiluna. Based on available evidence, the decline would seem to have been partly due to economic and ecological reasons. "By the beginning of the 17th century," as American archaeologists James A. Armstrong and Margaret Catlin Brandt have observed, "literate, urbanized Babylonia was restricted to the northwestern corner of the alluvial plain, the region just to the north and south of the city of Babylon. The great cities of the south were essentially dead."

In the estimation of many scholars, a slow, westward shift in the flow of the Euphrates through the middle of the southern plains had brought disaster, reducing the volume of water that entered its channels and the numerous canals that had been cut through the fields. Keeping these open and free of silt—and extending them as necessary—was an ever-present challenge for the Mesopotamians, and any change in the river's flow only added to the gravity of the task. "Without sufficient river water for irrigation," explains Armstrong, "the cities along the old channels died." Once-productive farmland dried up, the urban heart of Babylonia was depopulated, and

This 1300-BC clay map of Nippur, found during an excavation of the city in 1899, has proved remarkably accurate when compared with modern aerial photographs of the area. The square in the top right-hand corner is Nippur's ziggurat; running from the north to the southeast is a canal that cut through the middle of the city; and to the west is the Euphrates.

An aerial shot of an excavation at Nippur gives an idea of the conditions archaeologists face in this part of the world. Windblown dust, which can infill sites as quickly as they are excavated, is one of the most vexing problems. Sandstorms, snakes, scorpions, hunting spiders, and sandflies are other hazards the diggers face.

Babylonia itself settled into a period so lacking in historical and archaeological remains that scholars have referred to it as a dark age.

Though disaster was perhaps inevitable as the river naturally shifted course, it may have been hastened by direct human intervention. Several scientists have speculated that the water flow might have been manipulated for military purposes. With the hegemony of Babylon, it is argued, political power lay for the first time in the hands of a city that could control all the southern watercourses and therefore use water as a weapon.

This ecological warfare allegedly begins with Samsuiluna, although small-scale water diversion had been used as a military weapon for centuries. About nine years into his reign, in 1742 BC, Ur joined Larsa and other cities in the southern part of Babylonia in a rebellion against Babylon's supremacy. Within two years, however, the alliance was defeated. As part of his campaign, Samsuiluna may somehow have diverted or retarded the flow of those channels that fed his enemies' fields in order to force his foes into submission. It is also possible that the turmoil associated with the rebellion resulted in a failure to maintain the dams needed to keep the westward-trending Euphrates in its accustomed beds.

Samsuiluna marked his victory by naming the 11th year of his reign "the year in which Samsuiluna destroyed the walls of Ur and Uruk." Texts indicate life in the defeated cities continued somewhat normally for a year or so, but in 1740 BC, Ur, Larsa, and the other rebellious cities of southern Babylonia were abruptly abandoned.

At Nippur, however, and the other centrally located cities that lay upstream between Babylonia and Ur, a reduction in the waters entering the channels in the north near Babylon would have been a significant but not fatal change. Interestingly, cuneiform records indicate that at this time the less well-off inhabitants of Nippur began selling their land in droves to rich speculators and leaving their homes. Something unusual was going on. Tablets from Nippur reveal how around 1739 BC land sales soared as the price of land plunged. The diverted waters, perhaps, were not returning as quickly and bountifully as anticipated following the rebellion.

To avert further disaster, Samsuiluna may have managed to reestablish the normal flow to the central area, for by 1730 BC, Nippur and the midland cities were again prospering. But Ur and the southern cities remained uninhabited. Both archaeological and textual data from some of the northern cities provide a clue to what happened to the population of these southern centers. In northern Babylonia, what were once small towns now grew to urban status, and many of the names of their inhabitants betray their southern origins.

Ten years later, in 1720 BC, another insurrection occurred. The new uprising was supported by Nippur and most of the remaining cities in central Babylonia. In this instance, these cities were abandoned before the rebellion was two years old, again presumably because they lacked water. As a result of this coincidence—not once but twice—between rebellion and urban abandonment, some scholars believe that the root cause must have been the deliberate diversion of water for short-term political ends. But the abandonment of first southern and then central Babylonia would not have been in Samsuiluna's interest either economically or symbolically. He would have lost not only the most productive part of his kingdom, but also prestige: Babylonian kings were supposed to protect and preserve the sacred places, not preside over their demise. It seems likely that such actions would inadvertently have hastened the natural shift in the bed of the Euphrates to the west and that Samsuiluna lacked the engineering and organizational ability to reverse this process.

The cities of southern and central Babylonia were destined to remain ghost towns for centuries, a fact confirmed by recent strati-

A horned, serpentlike beast coils around the base of this 21-inch-high kudurru, *or boundary stone, that represented a grant of land by a king during the period of Kassite rule. To indicate divine approval of such royal transactions, the pillar-shaped stones carried emblems of the gods and stern warnings for those who disregarded the field boundaries.*

graphic studies showing that sand dunes grew up and gradually advanced over the remains of Nippur and its surrounding area.

During this time the region was beset by yet another kind of disaster when a new group of intruders, the Kassites, descended from their homeland, thought to be in the Zagros Mountains, onto the Mesopotamian plain in a continuous and generally peaceful influx. They make their first appearance in Babylonian documents only nine years after Hammurabi's death, during Samsuiluna's difficult reign. The Babylonian king apparently rebuffed an initial Kassite incursion, but over the next 150 years his successors faced increased emigration from the north.

Throughout the 17th century BC, Kassite names crop up frequently in Babylonian business documents, an indication that the Kassites, like the Amorites before them, had started to win acceptance for themselves. In time, most of the newcomers would quietly coexist with the population at large, earning their keep as farm laborers and mercenaries. It may even be that feuding dynastic leaders from Mesopotamian families of long pedigree, in times of crisis, had invited outsiders such as Kassites in as mediators and perhaps figurehead rulers. Though initially the influx of numerous Kassites may have brought instability to Mesopotamian society, there were also benefits. Stone argues that, like the Amorites before them, these immigrants contributed to the region's revitalization.

The story of Old Babylonia ended when mighty Babylon—the conqueror of so many other city-states—fell to a Hittite army around 1595 BC. The Hittites, who lived in Anatolia in what is now eastern Turkey, overwhelmed and looted the city in a lightning strike, which was followed by an equally precipitous withdrawal as the victors rushed home to put down a palace revolt. They never returned to capitalize on their conquest. But the damage had been done, and among the casualties was Babylon's dynastic kingship. Into the resulting political vacuum later stepped the Kassites to begin their own dynasty. By 1460 BC, most of Babylonia was under their control.

It was, in fact, the Kassites who ultimately restored, some 300 years after their desertion, Ur and the other abandoned cities, still revered even if long dead. American archaeologist Robert McCormick Adams, who would later become director of the Smithsonian Institution in Washington, D.C., used surface surveys of southern Babylonia and aerial photographs to draw up maps demonstrating that by the late 14th century BC, the orientation of the canals fed by the Euphrates and its channels had changed. It seems not only that new canals had been built but also that they no longer followed the natural slope of the alluvial plain. Instead, they cut transversely across the slope in an effort to bring water from the river's wandering course to the reviving towns. The building of these canals was a giant undertaking, one that required the enormous resources of a stable Kassite kingdom to keep them from silting up even as new canals were being dug. It was not new technology that enabled the Kassites to resuscitate the old cities, but a thriving economy and a large, submissive population that could be drafted for the enormous job of building and maintenance.

While thousands of Kassite texts have been found, they remain unedited, and little is known of the four centuries of Kassite hegemony. The surviving city-states apparently did not try to break away or form rival empires, which was perhaps a tribute to the Kassites' judicious governance and many building projects in these cities. Whatever the Kassite merits, the scene now shifts northward to Assyria where, in the 15th century BC, a new Mesopotamian culture would arise, to document its remarkable story in scribal clay.

TOWER OF HEAVEN AND EARTH

The biblical story of the Tower of Babel has held people in thrall since it was first told. But did such a tower ever really exist, or was the multistoried structure merely a symbol of folly in a moral fable? The Book of Genesis describes how the Tower of Babel came to be. At a time "when the whole earth was of one language," the wandering descendants of Noah settled down on a plain and decided to "make us a name" by building themselves "a city and a tower, whose top may reach unto heaven. And the Lord came down to see the city and the tower, which the children of men builded." Troubled by their audacity, the Lord mixed up the language of the people so they no longer could understand one another, and he then scattered them throughout the world. "Therefore is the name of it called Babel because the Lord did there confound the language of all the earth."

Interestingly, *babel* is a Hebrew word that derives from *babili*, or "gate of god," the ancient Akkadian designation for Babylon. Whoever wrote the passage from Genesis apparently connected *babel*, perhaps in a play on words, with the Hebrew *balal*, meaning "to mix or confuse." Whether the author knew of an actual tower standing in Babylon is not known—but there was most definitely a tower. It was built originally by Hammurabi, rebuilt by King Nabopolassar, and later improved by Nabopolassar's son Nebuchadnezzar.

For centuries the biblical account of the Tower of Babel captured the imaginations of artists, as the above medieval illumination and the vivid scenes on the following pages show. Their work and the Bible itself impelled European travelers to seek it out. But when archaeologists finally identified Babylon's tower, they were in for something of a surprise.

The weathered hulk of the ziggurat of the vanished 14th-century-BC Kassite city of Dur Kurigalzu climbs 188 feet from re-stored enclosure walls outside Baghdad. Some early travelers believed this to be the Tower of Babel. The striations are layers of reed matting and braided rope placed by the builders between every seven courses of mud brick for the purposes of bonding, draining, and leveling them.

Like a cone-shaped volcano, an unfinished
Tower of Babel looms in the middle of a
landscape more European than Mesopotamian in this 16th-century Flemish painting. In the right foreground, the biblical
builder King Nimrod and his architects
oversee construction. Babylon's tower
soared 300 feet into the sky; Nebuchadnezzar saw its height as rivaling heaven.

Though also placed in an imaginary
landscape, the multitiered Tower of Babel
in the 17th-century Flemish work below
looks more like the rectangular-based
ziggurats of ancient Mesopotamia than
the conical version in the painting at
left does. The artist portrayed it as
having many stories; the Greek historian
Herodotus claimed Babylon's tower rose in
eight stages, with a path winding around
the mass to a temple on top.

God's wrath is unleashed on Babylon in this 19th-century English mezzotint. Here lightning strikes the tower in 539 BC as people flee the Persians, seen with their war elephants battling the defenders beside the Euphrates River. Visiting the city's ruins in 323 BC, Alexander the Great sought to restore the tower and spent 60 days having rubble removed from the precincts around it. Alexander planned to make Babylon his eastern capital, but he died there before he could realize his dream.

Silhouetted against the evening sky, the ziggurat of Birs Nimrud near Babylon dominates the surrounding desert with its 154-foot height. This ruin, too, was mistaken for the tower by early travelers, who thought that the vitrified bricks at its top and lying at its base, hardened perhaps by lightning strikes, were evidence of God's vengeance. Taking note of the crevice running through the ziggurat, a 12th-century Spanish rabbi became convinced "fire from heaven split it to its very depth."

When studied in the early 20th century by the German archaeologist Robert Koldewey, Babylon's tower turned out to be the waterlogged ditch that traces the 300-foot-square base and grand staircase. Over the centuries, the tower had been dismantled for its bricks until almost none remained.

This reconstruction of the tower and temple, seen from on high, was based on Koldewey's work as well as on an ancient tablet describing its dimensions. Subsequent analysis by a German engineer, Hansjörg Schmid, suggests seven better-defined stages and longer stairways than those shown here.

Inspired by Koldewey's Babylonian excavations, German archaeologist Walter Andrae created this 1923 pastel of a dreamy evening in the venerable city, with the 300-foot-tower rising above the walls of the Temple of Marduk, the city's chief god.

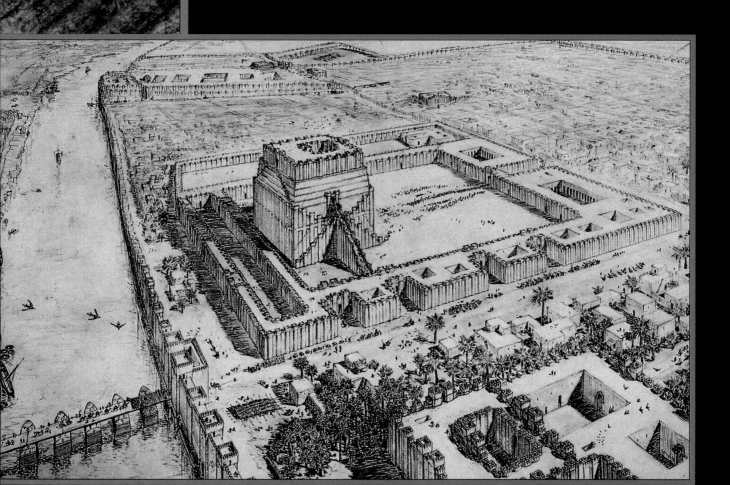

RUMBLINGS
OF A
SLEEPING GIANT

Sometime around 1900 BC, the king of Assur on the upper Tigris decided to crack down on smuggling by Assyrian merchants of his northern Mesopotamian city-state living in Anatolia. He was trying to placate the local rulers of that region, who had decreed that certain precious commodities not be traded like ordinary merchandise. Among these treasured products was iron, known as "the metal from heaven," presumably because it was recovered in meteoric form—the process of smelting the metal from ore had not yet been invented. So rare was iron in the Bronze Age that it traded for eight times the value of gold.

Alarmed by this turn of events, an Assyrian merchant sent a warning inscribed on a clay tablet to his associate in an Anatolian city called Kanesh in what is today modern Turkey. "Please do not smuggle anything," he beseeched him. "If you pass through Timilkia [one of the principalities along the trade route] leave your iron which you are bringing through in a friendly house, and leave one of your lads whom you trust, and come through yourself and we can discuss it here." He told of the plight of a merchant who had been caught with contraband by "the palace" and jailed. "Lookouts have been appointed," he cautioned.

There is no indication of how the situation was resolved, but almost 4,000 years later, in the early 1880s AD, many letters, of which

Wide, almond-shaped eyes stare from a vivid mask made of faience and adorned with glass beads by an artisan around 1300 BC. It was found in Karana, an Assyrian city that has provided striking examples of ancient glassmaking.

this is just one, began to appear in the antiquities market of Kayseri, a town in central Turkey. Dealing mostly with transactions between traders of Kanesh and Assyria, the letters were written in a type of cuneiform as unfamiliar to the scholars attempting to read them as the mysterious city to which they referred. But once the scholars realized that what they were confronting was an archaic version of the Assyrian dialect of Akkadian, the common language of Mesopotamia, they could begin to translate the texts. The researchers were surprised to discover that at this early stage in the development of Assyria, a half millennium before it would become a major power in Mesopotamia, Assyrians were already trading with people who lived 500 miles from their homeland—a two-month caravan journey over the Taurus Mountains. Almost nothing had hitherto been known about Assyria in the second millennium BC, when the tablets were written.

The tablets had a checkered history. The antiquities dealers of Kayseri were obtaining them from a small village a few miles outside of town. The source was thought to be a nearby hill that rose 60 feet above the local plain and was known locally as Kültepe, or "ash mound." Intrigued, a French explorer named Ernest Chantre attempted a preliminary excavation of the site in 1893. He found remnants of ancient buildings but failed to locate any tablets. Subsequent investigators fared no better, for the townspeople were reluctant to reveal their source to outsiders. Then in 1925 Bedrich Hrozny, a Czech archaeologist, reexamined the site. A local man serving as his party's cook led him to a spot about 100 yards to the northeast. Soon Hrozny was turning up tablet after tablet. From their contents, he realized that he had hit upon the remains of a merchants' quarter on the edge of Kanesh, where Assyrians—foreigners in an Anatolian city—had once lived and worked as representatives of merchant houses headquartered in Assur, the city from which the Assyrian empire would later derive its name.

Although the Kanesh letters show that, commercially at least, the Assyrians had unexpectedly broad horizons in this early phase of their history, designated as the Old Babylonian and Old Assyrian period (2000-1600 BC) by scholars, they were still fairly unsophisticated compared with the more formidable, urbane Babylonians living 750 miles to the south. Yet the Assyrians were destined for greatness. Their ascendance would begin during the Middle Assyrian period

A testament to the astonishing reach of early Assyria's trading caravans, the magnificent necklace at right, made around 1300 BC, includes blue cylinders of lapis lazuli imported from distant Afghanistan and orange carnelian beads from India. The necklace was unearthed in the ruins of the Assyrian capital of Assur, which lay on northern Mesopotamia's key trade route between the east and the Anatolian plateau of present-day Turkey.

(1600-1000 BC) and culminate in the first millennium BC, when the so-called Neo-Assyrians (1000-605 BC) would sweep through the Middle East like a whirlwind, toppling thrones and unsettling lives in their rush to empire.

Assyria had a great deal going for it. Unlike the south, it was blessed with such natural resources as stone, wood, and water. Where the Tigris and Euphrates diverged to create a 150-mile-wide area known today as al-Jazirah, "the Island," farmers could grow crops without recourse to irrigation. Indeed, grain fields and orchards still rim the rivers and dot the rolling landscape around the region's multiple springs and wells. And beyond lay a grass-covered steppe that even now provides spring pastures for livestock.

Such productive land seems to have attracted the attention of tribes from the Zagros Mountains to the east, peoples from the Euphrates basin to the west, and raiders from the northern highlands. Assyria had to be ever on the alert to guard against incursions by these groups. In addition, Assyria found itself engaged in frequent disputes with Babylonia.

The Kanesh letters reveal, however, that the earliest Assyrian rulers did not harbor the military ambitions of later kings. Their major interest was trade. Further investigation at Kanesh by Turkish archaeologists in the years following World War II has produced a flood of new information about the Assyrian colony there and the commerce that was its reason for existence. To date, more than 16,000 tablets have been exhumed, and they provide lively details concerning the extensive commercial links between northern Mesopotamia and Anatolia in the 19th century BC.

Donkey caravans carried cloth and loads of tin, required for bronze production, from Assur to Kanesh, where the goods were distributed to Assyrian merchant colonies scattered throughout Anatolia. The Assyrian merchants received payment in silver, or less commonly in gold, which they then sent back to Assur.

The goods and raw materials were not always Assyrian in origin. There are no tin mines in northern Mesopotamia, for example, and some of the textiles came from Babylon and were considered superior to Assyrian cloth by the Anatolians.

Evidently the Assyrians were serving as middlemen, import-export traders who made their profits on big markups—ranging from 100 to 600 percent. But like traders ever since, they saw their margins substantially eroded not only by customs duties, payable on shipments leaving Assur as well as on those arriving in Kanesh, but also by transit taxes amounting to about 10 percent of the goods' value, exacted by towns along the trade routes. Needless to say, so many impediments encouraged smuggling.

The picture of trade presented by the tablets is extraordinarily detailed. They indicate, for instance, that each donkey carried a 200-pound load. The tin, stored in packs with clay seals to prevent pilfering, hung in panniers on each side, while bundles of fabric, which had been sorted according to quality, were tied in bags to the beast's back. Although the cloth was mostly woven in temple workshops, some of it was produced by women working at home, who on occasion negotiated directly with the caravan drivers to transport their goods. Once packed, the caravan set out along a dangerous route where brigands might be waiting. But robbers seemed to have been less of a problem than the difficulties posed by nature, particularly in the mountains. Here, wolves and severe weather conditions threatened the convoys, and donkeys sometimes died on the way.

Most businesses were family run, with partnerships set up to provide the capital necessary to fund the ventures. In such cases collateral was essential, and loans were sometimes secured by the pledge of a man's entire estate, with his wife and children included. If he defaulted, his family would be sold into slavery to pay his debts.

The vividness of the Kanesh correspondence contrasts sharply with the great gaps in Assyria's history in the second millennium BC. Whole centuries pass by with barely an inscription to indicate its existence. One of the few continuous threads is the Assyrian King List. These records trace—with some inconsistency—what purports to be an unbroken line of 117 rulers of Assyria from the third millennium BC to the late eighth century BC. For the earliest, no more is known of them than their names. And at least 17 of the rulers who followed these obscure figures were nomadic tent dwellers, while others governed little more than their own small city-states.

The 39th monarch, Shamshi-Adad I of the late 19th, early 18th centuries BC, was among the first northern Mesopotamian kings with imperial aspirations. Of Amorite descent, he was the son of the ruler of a small principality on the middle Euphrates. In his youth, Shamshi-Adad visited Babylonia. After returning home, he launched a successful assault on Ekallatum, a fortress city east of the

Tigris and north of Assur, and remained there three years. From this base he turned his attention to the kingdom of Mari, about 150 miles southwest of Assur, which was apparently ripe for plucking around the beginning of the 18th century BC. Mari's king at the time, Iakhdunlim, appears to have met his death as a result of palace intrigue, perhaps at the hands of one of his own sons. Taking advantage of the ensuing chaos, Shamshi-Adad seized control of Mari and installed his younger and more irresponsible son, Yasmah-Adad, as his viceroy there. He then left his older son, Ishme-Dagan, in charge of Ekallatum, while he himself went on to take Assur. Victory followed victory until ultimately he extended his realm to include nearly all of northern Mesopotamia.

For his own capital Shamshi-Adad chose neither Assur nor Mari, settling instead on a city he named Shubat-Enlil. Its location has recently been identified as Tell Leilan, a site some 150 miles northwest of Assur near the headwaters of the Habur River, a tributary of the Euphrates, in what is today northeastern Syria. Excavations conducted there in the 1970s by an American team from Yale University have uncovered a metropolis 220 acres in extent whose walls still rise in places 50 feet above the surrounding plain. The capital was dominated by a 37-acre acropolis that included a temple and an adjacent structure in ziggurat form. Within the temple were the remains of columns decorated to resemble the trunks of palm trees.

During Shamshi-Adad's reign Assur, Nineveh, and Erbil were first brought under the control of a single monarch. To him, Assur owed the reconstruction of its great temple, built on a promontory dominating the city. Previously established for worshiping the Sumerian god Enlil, Shamshi-Adad rededicated it to the city-state's namesake deity, Assur.

Shamshi-Adad also founded new towns, some of them on the well-watered Jazirah plain between the Tigris and Euphrates. Most

Excavated walls of mud-brick dwellings border an ancient street—now punctured by modern wells—that runs left to right in an aerial photograph taken from a kite of the once imposing city of Shubat-Enlil, capital of the powerful Assyrian ruler Shamshi-Adad, who reigned from 1813 to 1781 BC. Located in today's Syria, the city at one time dominated the fertile, well-watered Habur plain, a vital source of Assyria's food through much of the empire's history.

of these so far remain unexplored. Excavations during the 1960s under the direction of British archaeologist David Oates at Tell al-Rimah, which lies some 60 miles northwest of Assur between the Tigris and the Euphrates, concentrated on the ruins of one of Shamshi-Adad's new cities. Known as Karana in ancient times, it was, in Oates's words, "a peaceful and moderately prosperous country town." Karana's temple, whose columns also show traces of the telling palm-trunk decorations, was planned on a scale that suggests the magnitude of Shamshi-Adad's ambitions.

Fortunately for scholars, the empire of Shamshi-Adad is richly documented, thanks to the royal archives discovered by André Parrot at Mari as well as some of the cuneiform tablets unearthed at the Assyrian merchant colony at Kanesh. These caches include numerous letters between Shamshi-Adad and his sons that illuminate not only the politics of the time but also strained relationships within the royal family itself.

Like feckless sons of every age, Mari's governor, Yasmah-Adad, was forever being chastised by his father for his idleness. "Are you a child, not a man?" Shamshi-Adad writes in response to some unrecorded incident at his son's court. "Have you no beard on your chin? Even now, when you have reached maturity, you have not set up a home. Who is there to look after your house?" In another letter Shamshi-Adad castigates his son for doing nothing but "reclining among the women" while his older brother, Ishme-Dagan, now governor of Assur, was out with his army, winning great victories for the empire. Still another letter finds the father wondering whether he will have to hold his younger son's administrative hand forever, even as the more responsible Ishme-Dagan is so ably commanding far-flung armies.

Stung, Yasmah-Adad was not so browbeaten that he was afraid to talk back to his father: "How can it be," he asks petulantly in response to one of his father's tirades, "that though I have

Four-thousand-year-old decorative columns made of mud brick and plaster adorn the massive outer walls of the great temple of Shubat-Enlil unearthed by archaeologists in the early 1980s. Most elaborate are spiral columns, made from preformed bricks, that twist in opposite directions; others found here but not shown resemble trunks of palms.

grown up with you, Daddy, ever since I was little, now some servant or other has succeeded in ousting me from my Daddy's affections?" Then, suddenly emboldened, Yasmah-Adad decides to take a more aggressive stance: "So I am coming to you right now, to have it out with you, Daddy, about my unhappiness." The outcome of the visit is unrecorded, but Yasmah-Adad kept his position as governor.

Given the tension between father and son, it is not surprising that the two siblings indulged in some rivalry of their own. In one letter to his brother, Assur's governor, Ishme-Dagan, is as reproachful as his father toward his ne'er-do-well younger sibling, exhorting Yasmah-Adad to stop his whining, and to shape up and act like a man. On another occasion, Ishme-Dagan upbraids his brother for overreacting to a local raid and putting the entire army on alert by activating the country's signal-fire alarm system, probably a chain of beacons, capable of transmitting a message of military emergency across the entire country. "Because you lit two fires during the night," Ishme-Dagan snaps at his brother, "it is possible that the whole land will be coming to your assistance."

In the end, however, neither brother would prove able to fill his father's sandals, and Shamshi-Adad's empire, which had been held together largely by the force of the ruler's personality, would begin to unravel in 1781 BC with his death. His older son, Ishme-Dagan, scarcely had time to warm his father's throne at Shubat-Enlil, Shamshi-Adad's capital, before losing the city to the Elamites of southern Iran, despite having assured his brother that he had the enemy "on a leash." As for the incompetent Yasmah-Adad, without his father's patronage, he soon found himself ousted from his post at Mari. He was replaced by Mari's last king, Zimrilim, Hammurabi's one-time friend and ally, who was the son of the previous ruler and thus had a legitimate claim to the throne.

When the light of history shines again on Assyria in the 15th century BC, it reveals an altered world. Now, two new empires compete for influence in the region, maintaining a delicate balance of power monitored through regular diplomatic contact with each oth-

A triumph of early Assyrian glassmaking, the handsome goblet above was molded of opaque glass, then decorated by an artisan who applied rods of partially melted colored glass to the vessel's still-soft surface and moved them up and down to create the zigzag pattern. The beaker was found during the British excavations at Tell al-Rimah, the huge mound in today's Iraq that holds remains of an Assyrian city dating back to the sixth millennium BC.

er and with the rulers of Egypt and Babylon. The older of these were the Hittites of Anatolia. By honing their military skills, the Hittites had become rivals of Egypt for political mastery of the Middle East. The Hittite capital of Hattusas stood 3,000 feet above the central Anatolian plain, about 90 miles east of the present-day Turkish capital, Ankara. The Hittites had already shown themselves to be a force in Mesopotamian politics at the start of the 16th century BC, when they conducted their raid on Babylon and left the mighty city defenseless against its foes.

Although the rulers of the northern Mesopotamian city-states must have been very conscious of the Hittite threat to them, they were more immediately affected by the other new power, which confronted them closer to home. This was the kingdom of Mitanni, largely populated by a people called the Hurrians.

The Hurrians were by no means newcomers to the area. From their northern homeland, perhaps in the trans-Caucasian highlands, they had begun drifting southward in the course of the third millennium BC. Scholars have traced their presence in Mesopotamia by counting Hurrian names on tablets found in various archives, a relatively easy task since the language of the Hurrians is very different from all other tongues spoken in the area, being neither Semitic nor

Sophisticated arches made of mud brick top a doorway of the Great Temple at Tell al-Rimah. Added in the 15th century BC, the arches are the earliest examples of true vaulting. The massive 18th-century-BC temple was erected by Shamshi-Adad in the center of the town, which scholars now believe was the trading city of Karana.

Indo-European in its derivation. The major part of the Hurrian population remained to the north of the Mesopotamian plain. By the time of Shamshi-Adad, a chain of Hurrian city-states stretched from northern Syria to the Zagros Mountains of present-day Iran; by its peak in the 15th century BC the kingdom of Mitanni grew, expanding to include Assur and what is now part of the Mediterranean littoral of present-day Turkey. The site of Mitanni's capital, Washukanni, has not yet been found, although the city is believed to have been on the Habur River plains, not far from Shamshi-Adad's capital, Shubat-Enlil.

The early years of the kingdom of Mitanni are still shrouded in mystery, and much of what is known about its subsequent history comes not from northern Mesopotamia but from Egypt. There a major cache of diplomatic correspondence was found in 1887 by an Egyptian peasant woman digging in a pile of refuse at Tell el-Amarna in central Egypt, site of the pharaoh Akhenaten's short-lived capital. From her village individual clay texts began turning up in the Cairo antiquities market.

News of what soon would become known as the Amarna letters reached Western scholars, one of whom was E. A. Wallis Budge of the Department of Oriental Antiquities at the British Museum. Whereas some scorned them as forgeries and others made no comment, Budge was intrigued, and he set off at once for Egypt to investigate. Unlike most of the Egyptologists of the day, who could read only hieroglyphics, Budge also had experience of cuneiform, which enabled him to confirm that the tablets were genuine. He subsequently managed to acquire some for the museum.

The Amarna tablets turned out to be part of the archive of international correspondence of the pharaohs Amenophis III and Akhenaten, written between the 15th and 14th centuries BC in Akkadian, which was not only the ancient tongue of Mesopotamia but also the diplomatic language of the time. Included were about 50 missives from Hittite, Babylonian, and Assyrian monarchs as well as from Mitannian kings. Scholars had not previously suspected the importance of the kingdom of Mitanni in the politics of the day, and the tablets profoundly altered then-current views of the ancient world. The writings showed the Mitannian and Egyptian rulers dealing on equal terms and contracting alliances. One Mitannian monarch who gave a daughter to the pharaoh Amenophis III in marriage felt sure enough of his position to request a golden statue of her in return so that, as he put it, he would not miss her.

Other letters reveal a king of Mitanni dispatching the statue of the fertility goddess Ishtar, renowned for its healing properties, from the temple of Nineveh to Egypt to help Amenophis recover from illness. Assur and the other northern cities were vassal states of Mitanni at the time, according to information gleaned from still another outstanding collection of tablets discovered by American archaeologists at Nuzi in northeastern Iraq between 1925 and 1931. Nuzi lies near modern Kirkuk, 60 miles from Assur, in the direction opposite that of the Mitannian kingdom. Yet the tablets demonstrate that its Akkadian-writing Mesopotamian citizens regarded themselves very much as subjects of Mitanni.

The ambitions of Assur's rulers may have lain dormant in the years of Mitannian overlordship, but the Amarna records indicate that they were never abandoned. Early in the 15th century BC an Assyrian king sent gifts of lapis lazuli and ornamental wood to the Egyptian court to congratulate the pharaoh Thutmose III on his capture of the Syrian town of Megiddo, an act suggesting that Assyria was still maintaining an independent foreign policy. By the end of that century the walls of Assur were rebuilt, and soon after a new boundary treaty was signed with the Babylonians. The Assyrians, it seems, were steadily advancing their own interests, ready to take advantage of any opportunity for expansion.

Such a possibility arose in the mid 14th century, when Mitanni was fatally weakened by factional infighting in the wake of the assassination of a king. In the ensuing civil war, one party sought help from neighboring powers, including the Hittites and a resurgent Assyria. Mitanni found itself under attack on several fronts, and it quickly succumbed under the pressure. Although its people would remain an important group in the Middle East for centuries to come, the kingdom was all but destroyed. Within decades its eastern lands had become an Assyrian province, while the western territories were absorbed into the Hittite realm. Only a small rump state survived into the following century.

The acquisition of Mitanni's lands signaled the beginning of the first period of Assyrian expansion. Known as the Middle Assyrian era, it was a time of territorial growth under the leadership of a series of strong monarchs, matched by intervening periods of withdrawal under less effective kings.

Yet even a weak Assyrian ruler had a readily available pool of yeoman to conscript into the army, for military duties fit conveniently into the annual agricultural cycle. The harvest was brought in during the early summer, leaving the farmers who made up the greater part of the nation's population temporarily free for active service at a season when the mountain passes were clear of snow. The kings took

A rare relic of the mysterious Hurrian people, the small but magnificent cast-bronze figure of a snarling lion at left tapers at its bottom into a simple peg, indicating it was driven into the foundation of a building as magic protection against evildoers. The lion's outsize paws rest on a plate inscribed in the Hurrian language with the name of Tishatal, known to have been a king of Urkish, a Hurrian city-state on the northern edge of Mesopotamia.

advantage of this availability to organize annual raids into the Zagros highlands to subdue the tribes that posed a continuing threat to their land. More ambitious incursions were also undertaken into the prosperous and settled lands to the west. Here, unlike in the mountain forays, there was always the risk of clashing with the troops of a powerful rival, primarily the Hittites.

The ruler who set Assyria on the path of widespread conquest was Ashuruballit I, who ascended the throne in 1365 BC. This monarch managed to annex from the collapsing Mitannian kingdom the rich farming lands to the north and west of Assur that would remain the heartland of the Assyrian empire for the next seven centuries. Conscious of his enhanced status, he felt sure enough of his position to send an envoy to Egypt with a view to establishing diplomatic relations. "I have sent my envoy to you," Ashuruballit wrote to the pharaoh Akhenaten, "to see you and to see your land. I have entered into communication with you today as up to this time my forefathers never entered into communication."

The visit, which was sweetened by presents of a chariot and of lapis lazuli jewelry, seems to have been successful, because a second letter, also recovered from the Amarna archives, refers to Egyptian envoys being entertained at the Assyrian court. In return for further gifts, Ashuruballit requests the dispatch of a substantial amount of gold to decorate a palace he was building, pointing out that gold "is like dust in the land of Egypt."

Such presumption on the part of the ruler of a newly independent power did not go unnoticed by Assyria's neighbors. A letter from the king of Babylon seems to suggest that the southern monarch may have entertained hopes of succeeding the vanquished kingdom of Mitanni as Assyria's overlord at this time. He complains to the pharaoh that the envoys should never have been dispatched: "Now it was not I who sent the Assyrians, my own subjects, to you; they act according to their own decisions. Why did they travel to your country? If you care for me, they must not do any buying there; chase them away empty-handed!"

This glazed terra-cotta head of a boar was made about 1350 BC in the Hurrian city of Nuzi in today's Iraq. Such pigs may have been domesticated far earlier than once believed. Huge deposits of 10,000-year-old pig bones, recently discovered in the ruins of ancient villages in the Taurus Mountains of today's eastern Turkey, bolster the theory that swine were domesticated even before sheep and goats.

But in fact the Babylonian claim to overlordship proved unenforceable, and by the end of Ashuruballit's reign the balance of power between these neighboring states had tipped decisively in favor of Assyria, through a series of shifting alliances. Ashuruballit had forged a marriage alliance by sending one of his daughters to the Babylonian king. When the son of this match was subsequently dethroned and killed by a rebel faction, the Assyrian king invaded Babylon to avenge his grandchild. Ashuruballit succeeded in deposing the usurper and placing a ruler of his own choice on the throne of Babylon. By the time of his death in 1328 BC, Ashuruballit had established Assyria as a major force in the region, second in influence only to the Hittites.

Ashuruballit's successors continued his military policies with varying degrees of effectiveness. His great-grandson Adad-Nirari I (1305-1275 BC) took to identifying himself on inscriptions as King of the Universe. He also had the temerity to write to the powerful Hittite ruler, addressing him as "My brother," as if they were on equal terms. The presumption earned a stinging rebuke. "Why should I write to you about brotherhood?" the Hittite monarch replied. "Were you and I born of the same mother?"

For all their pride, the Hittite kings felt threatened by the ascent of Assyria, and fear of this upstart may well have been the reason behind Hittite participation in a mutual nonaggression pact. By the terms of a treaty signed in 1269 BC, Ramses II of Egypt and the Hittite king Hattusilis III each agreed to come to the other's assistance in the event of an attack by a third party. Other measures against Assyria taken by the Hittite king included economic sanctions: A letter to the governor of a vassal state in Syria specifies that "no merchant of yours shall go to Assyria, and you shall allow no merchant of theirs into your land." Even so, the rising power's stature could no longer be denied; surviving diplomatic correspondence shows this same Hittite ruler consenting, unlike his predecessor, to address his Assyrian counterpart as "brother."

By this stage the Assyrian kings were already displaying the ferocity for which they were to be particularly remembered. Shalmaneser I (1275-1244 BC) introduced a policy, popular with later rulers, of transporting prisoners-of-war to Assyria for resettlement, usually to work in forced-labor gangs. Shalmaneser's consignment of prisoners consisted of 14,400 people from the Mitannian lands. To ensure their docility, he first had them blinded, an inscription records, although some scholars argue that they may have had only one eye put out in order to preserve their productive value.

The son of Shalmaneser, Tukulti-Ninurta I, was another highly skilled military leader. He carried out the usual campaigns against the Zagros mountain tribes, but with such success that he was able by his own count to bring 40 chiefs back to his capital with chains around their necks; the chiefs were later allowed to return to their former realms as Assyrian vassals.

Tukulti-Ninurta would be remembered, however, for another campaign that, although victorious, would ultimately lead to his downfall. He invaded Babylonia and in 1225 BC utterly defeated the forces of its Kassite ruler, Kashtiliash IV. In the words of one of his victory inscriptions, "I trod on his royal neck with my feet like a footstool. I brought him stripped and bound before Assur my lord. Sumer and Akkad to its farthest border I brought under my sway. On the lower sea of the rising sun [the Persian Gulf] I established the frontier of my land."

In the face of his triumphs, the Assyrian king made a grievous error—that of transporting the statue of the god Marduk from Babylon to Assur as part of the spoils of war. Although Marduk was the patron deity of Babylon, he was also revered throughout the Mesopotamian world, and Tukulti-Ninurta's temerity in removing the image was seen by many of his own subjects as sacrilege. One of the first known Assyrian literary works, an epic describing the Babylon campaign, set out deliberately to refute such ideas. It emphasized Tukulti-Ninurta's initial reluctance to go to war, even though he had been provoked by the Babylonians who had raided Assyria. The text asserted that Marduk in fact had abandoned the Babylonian king by refusing to supply him with propitious omens.

Within seven years, the people of Babylon successfully rebelled against the puppet ruler that Tukulti-Ninurta had placed on

THE WORLD'S FIRST GREAT EPIC POEM

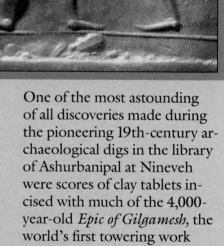

One of the most astounding of all discoveries made during the pioneering 19th-century archaeological digs in the library of Ashurbanipal at Nineveh were scores of clay tablets incised with much of the 4,000-year-old *Epic of Gilgamesh,* the world's first towering work of literature.

Telling the saga of a king of the early Sumerian city of Uruk, the great poem recounts how the hero Gilgamesh becomes fast friends with his erstwhile rival, Enkidu. Together the two set out to kill a loathsome monster known as Humbaba, causer of fire, flood, and pestilence. Coming upon Humbaba in a distant cedar forest, the two men slay the monster, a scene so famous in the ancient Mesopotamian world that artists portrayed it over and over in carvings and seals such as the one shown here, thought to picture Gilgamesh, second from left, about to decapitate Humbaba while a bearded Enkidu helps.

Flushed with victory, the friends return to Uruk, where Gilgamesh has the audacity to reject a marriage proposal from the goddess Ishtar. In revenge, Ishtar sends down the great Bull of Heaven to do him in. Once more Gilgamesh and Enkidu destroy their adversary. For the sacrilege of killing a deity, however, Enkidu must pay with his life.

Gilgamesh, sick with grief and with the fear of his own mortality, exiles himself from Uruk and wanders on a long and harrowing trek through the Middle East, surviving many perils—and hearing the story of a great flood that, like the deluge in the Bible, almost wiped out humankind.

Finally becoming reconciled to the fact that all people must eventually die, Gilgamesh returns to his home of Uruk, where—now a wise and moderate ruler—he takes comfort in building a magnificent wall that will protect his city and its inhabitants throughout his benevolent reign.

the throne, and a faction in the Assyrian capital chose to see the Babylonian victory as a sign of divine retribution against the Assyrian king. His fate is laconically recorded in a chronicle, "Tukulti-Ninurta, who had brought his hand for evil upon Babylon: His son Ashurnasirpal and the nobles of Assur rebelled against him, removed him from his throne, imprisoned him in a building in Kar-Tukulti-Ninurta, and killed him with a weapon."

The upheavals and uncertainties that followed Tukulti-Ninurta's assassination were only part of the greater chaos that seemed to be overtaking the world around this time. Among other things, the balance of power in the Middle East was radically altered with the capture and destruction of Hattusas, the Hittite capital, effected by unknown aggressors around 1200 BC and with the subsequent collapse of the Hittite empire, which had spread across the Anatolian plateau down into the Levant. The attack on the Hittite capital seems to have been part of the widespread unrest and instability associated with the displacement and movement of peoples that afflicted the Middle East during this time. The period was marked by the arrival of the mysterious Sea Peoples and by a seaborne assault on Egypt beaten off by Ramses III's ships in one of history's first recorded naval battles. The political map of the Mediterranean littoral was about to be redrawn.

A major step forward in understanding this and other periods of Assyrian history was taken in 1903 when German archaeologists embarked on what would turn out to be a 10-year dig at Assur, under the leadership of Walter Andrae (pages 64-65), who had worked on an earlier excavation of Babylon directed by Robert Koldewey.

Andrae and his team went about their tasks precisely and efficiently, making good use of the techniques developed through the experiences of nearly a century of archaeologists and adventurers. They began by digging exploratory trenches at 100-yard intervals across the heights on which they believed the central, monumental section of the city had been built. When this indeed proved to be the case, they then turned their attention to tracing the full circuit of the surrounding fortifications.

Most valuable of all from the historian's point of view, Andrae and his team found numerous cuneiform writings at Assur. Some were carved on walls, others impressed onto clay tablets. Mentioned in these writings were 38 places of worship, of which Andrae managed to excavate four. Among the most revealing of the texts was an incomplete set of Middle Assyrian laws, dealing specifically with issues of land tenure and with the role of women. These writings, taken together with the Nuzi tablets uncovered by an American team in the 1920s and with inscriptions found at other sites, make it possible to develop an idea of what life was like in Mesopotamia during the Middle Assyrian period.

In contrast to the city-dwelling inhabitants of Babylonia, the population of Assyria generally worked on the land and lived in and around villages that were linked, for taxation purposes, to the major urban centers of Assur, Nineveh, and Erbil. Census records from the first millennium BC indicate that the typical household consisted of a couple with one or more offspring; the statistical average works out to 1.43 children per home, although this figure would not have included those youngsters who had died, set up households of their own, or departed on state service. A single wife was the rule, although nothing except the expense involved prevented a farmer from having more than one spouse.

Land originally had been held in common by extended families or entire villages. By the Middle Assyrian period, however, it had mostly fallen into the hands of the rich. The labor of serfs could be bought or sold with the land they worked, but otherwise they retained basic citizens' rights. The slave class at the bottom of the social ladder included individuals who had fallen into debt and had been compelled to surrender themselves (and often their families) into the hands of creditors. The lot of slaves was brutal: The laws specifically permitted their master to beat them, and they could be sold at will, even to a buyer from outside Assyria.

Assyria had some fairly decent farm country, so work on the land was not in itself particularly demanding. The principal crops were barley and wheat, though emmer and millet were also common. The agricultural year began in the fall with ploughing and sowing, and farmers then anxiously scanned the skies for clouds, for if the rain was long delayed, crop failure could ensue. Another potential danger was the sudden appearance of locust swarms, though in that case people sought some compensation for lost crops by catching and eating the insects, which were considered a delicacy.

The harvest was gathered in May or June with the aid of copper or bronze sickles. After being cleaned, the grain was stored in warehouses before being ground into flour for bread or crushed for use as groats; barley was also instrumental in making beer. Other foodstuffs grown by the Assyrians at this time included lentils, chickpeas, cucumbers, pomegranates, olives, grapes, and figs, and dates were imported from Babylonia. Farmers also kept livestock—cattle, sheep, and goats—while pigs roamed the streets freely as scavengers, providing Assyrian towns with the nearest thing they possessed to a refuse disposal system. Although pork was eaten by the Assyrians in earlier centuries, after 1400 BC a taboo against its consumption would gradually develop, perhaps in response to the threat of trichinosis from infected meat, a stricture still observed among Muslims in the region and elsewhere today.

The towns were centers of commerce where deals were paid for by barter arrangements or in precious metals such as gold, silver, copper, bronze, tin, or some combination of them. There is a record, for instance, of construction workers receiving a daily wage of six pounds of bread and six pints of beer, plus a measured amount of copper. Unsurprisingly, the need to weigh out all such payments led to suspicions about the accuracy of the measuring devices; one tablet complains of the practices of the dishonest tradesman who "as he holds the balance, indulges in cheating by substituting weights."

Prices were apparently set by the market rather than by government edict, for contracts sometimes specified that goods should be paid for according to the going price at the time of settlement. Then as now business activity was cyclical, and astrologers and diviners tried to forecast future trends. One surviving text claims that "When the moon appears at a time not expected for it, business activity will be reduced"; another text reads that when there was a fog in the land, "the harvest will be abundant, trade will be firm."

Of the multitude of writings uncovered, among the most

Paying homage to the written word, the 13th-century-BC Assyrian king Tukulti-Ninurta I appears twice in the remarkable stone carving below found at Assur, first standing (left) and then kneeling, as he worships before the altar of the writing god, Nabu. The god's altar, fittingly enough, is topped by a stylus and tablet, and its shape copies exactly that of the whole monument, which was itself intended for acts of worship.

BRINGING ASSUR BACK TO LIFE

Trained in Dresden as an architect and a skilled artist, the brilliant German excavator Walter Andrae not only perfected modern scientific methods of excavation while unearthing the city of Assur, but also produced matchless pictures of what the Assyrian capital probably looked like 3,000 years ago. Hundreds of these detailed drawings and paintings, two of them reproduced here, flowed from Andrae's desk throughout his marathon excavations, from 1904 to 1914, vividly recreating Assur's walls, fortifications, and temples, and its busy riverfront on the Tigris. Retiring from fieldwork after World War I, Andrae became the revered and influential director of the Near Eastern sections of the Berlin Museum. He died, much honored for his lifetime's work, in 1956 at age 81.

Trading craft cluster by a quay on the Tigris below Assur's looming walls in one of Andrae's detailed reconstructions of the city as it looked about 1210 BC. Above is a self-portrait done by a young Andrae in 1902 when he was helping his great mentor Robert Koldewey explore Babylon.

Viewed across the Tigris, Assur's main ziggurat towers above the mass of the city's other public buildings in another of Andrae's drawings. At right a photograph shows the ruins of the ziggurat as they look in modern times, highlighting Andrae's astonishing ability to reconstruct with his architect's eye—and archaeologist's instincts—the great shapes that once rose above the crumbling piles of brick that are Assur today.

fascinating are those bearing on the intimacies of Assyrian domestic life. Within the home, Assyrian society was fiercely patriarchal. All authority was vested in the male head of the household, who exercised dictatorial power over his wife and children. A wife was, by law, the chattel of her husband. The general attitude toward wives is summed up succinctly by the final clause of the laws relating to women, which outlines a husband's right to punish his spouse for offenses not otherwise covered by its provisions. Apart from the penalties for a married woman that are written on the tablet, it specifies that, when she is thought to deserve it, "a man may flog his wife, he may pull out her hair, he may damage and split her ears, with no liability attaching to him."

The lowly status of women was clearly manifested in Assyrian attitudes toward divorce. A husband could leave his wife simply by cutting off the hem of her garment before official witnesses. In such cases the man was not—contrary to the practice in Babylon—obliged to provide compensation; the wife retained the right only to the bridal gifts she had brought at the time of the marriage. Yet a woman had no equivalent power; indeed, merely expressing a desire for a divorce could be enough to have her put out of her husband's house naked and penniless.

Other forms of misbehavior were punished still more harshly. The range of sanctions invoked by the Assyrian legal code included, besides the death sentence, blinding, flogging with staves, and various forms of mutilation including the cutting off of noses, ears, lips, or fingers. Women who caused themselves to miscarry were impaled on stakes. Men who falsely accused their neighbors or their wives of adultery were liable to castration.

To modern eyes, a particularly repellent aspect of these Assyrian laws is the way in which a man's wife or daughter could be forced to pay the penalty for his wrongdoings. For example, one clause specifies that if a man were to strike someone else's wife in such a way as to cause her to miscarry, the assailant's wife should then be assaulted in a similar manner.

The code regulating sexual behavior contains strictures that seem even more bizarre. The punishment for the rape of a virgin was that the assailant's wife should in turn be raped and taken away from her husband; the victim's father could then insist that the attacker marry his daughter. Prostitution played an accepted part in Assyrian life. Prostitutes and female slaves were distinguished by the fact that

Meticulously reconstructed from fragments found in a major temple at Assur, a monumental stone relief portrays a majestic deity—a fertility god or perhaps the city's great patron, Assur himself— wearing a high headdress and holding in each hand long-stalked plants that are nibbled on by a pair of goats. At the god's side stand two women, possibly goddesses, who hold so-called fertility jugs from which pour streams of water.

they were obliged to keep their faces uncovered in public; respectable women were required to wear a veil. A prostitute seen veiled on the street risked a punishment of 50 strokes with a rod and having hot pitch poured over her. A slave girl committing the same offense fared even worse; she might have her ears cut off.

Not surprising in so partriarchal a society, citizens submitted themselves readily to the ruler. Ordinary people were not permitted to look at the monarch but were blindfolded before being escorted into his presence. The king's own family was also kept at bay; even the crown prince was allowed an audience with the king only when the omens were thought to be auspicious. Justification for such protectiveness lay in the ruler's status as the representative of the gods on earth. To placate his divine masters, the king was expected to fast regularly and to go on retreat to a crude reed hut; other rituals required the ruler to wear special religious garments or to remain indoors for several days at a time.

Omens dictated much of the monarch's activity, and to interpret them the king relied on an entourage of priests, diviners, astrologers, and soothsayers. The most serious of all the astrological portents affecting royalty was a solar or lunar eclipse, thought to foreshadow the death of a monarch. In such cases the reigning king would briefly abdicate, and a surrogate ruler would take his place for 100 days. At the end of that period the substitute would be executed, satisfactorily fulfilling the astrologers' predictions while allowing the true king to remount the throne unscathed.

For lesser mortals too, astrology and divination were a vital part of life. More than a quarter of the works in the most celebrated of all Assyrian archives, the library of the seventh-century-BC king Ashurbanipal at Nineveh, 75 miles north of Assur along the Tigris, were devoted to these arts.

The Nineveh tablets, excavated in the mid 19th century by Austen Henry Layard and others, described the popular divining technique of inspecting livers of sacrificial animals in search of the telltale signs and abnormalities used to predict the future. Practitioners of the art had clay models of the organs to guide them in their forecasts. Other methods of divination included ecstatic prophecy and the interpretation of dreams, as well as observation of heavenly bodies, changes in weather, and the behavior of birds. The diviners' practice of looking up explanations for astrological phenomena in ancient cuneiform texts occasionally allowed for alternative, vastly differing interpretations: "When a halo surrounds the Moon and Scorpio stands within it, this means either that priestesses will have intercourse with men or that lions will ravage and block the roads of the land."

Divination also played a central part in Assyrian medicine. Most illnesses were blamed on malign supernatural beings, among them Lamashtu, a female demon held responsible for Assyria's high infant-mortality rates. Lamashtu, a magical text had it, "keeps going after women about to give birth." To counter the activities of this terrible creature and her fellows, patients had recourse to shamans known as *ashipu*, who specialized in theatrical forms of exorcism. In a letter addressed to his monarch, one leading ashipu described the appropriate treatment for what seems to have been an attack of epilepsy: "The ashipu shall get up and hang a mouse and a twig of camel thorn on the lintel of the door. The ashipu shall dress in red clothing, and put on a red mask. He shall hold a raven in his right hand, a falcon in his left hand." Thus attired and equipped, the magician proposed to recite incantations while an assistant circled the bed of the invalid carrying a censer and a torch. The performance was to be repeated morning and evening until a cure was effected.

Alongside the practitioners of this kind of healing magic were less-prestigious figures known as *asu*, physicians who practiced a form of medicine that would be much more recognizable to today's patients. Herbs and plant extracts formed the bases of many of their cures, although there are also records of odder medications, among them milk in which a lizard had been boiled.

By the 12th century BC, this superstitious, order-loving Assyrian society was encountering fresh threats along its northern and western borders, where new groups of people were moving in to fill the open spaces left by the collapse of the Mitannian and Hittite realms. Nomadic Aramean tribesmen had thrust eastward from the Syrian desert and had settled along the length of the Euphrates River, forming a network of small kingdoms that threatened to throttle the established Mesopotamian powers. And from the northwest came the Mushku, possibly an Indo-European people who seized territory in southern Asia Minor that the Assyrians considered among their own provinces.

Fortunately for Assyria, a new military leader of genius ascended the throne in 1115 BC to confront the rising menace. Tiglath-Pileser I started off his aggressive reign by attacking the Mushku. He won back the disputed terrain and celebrated his victory with an exhibit of the heads of Mushku leaders on the Nineveh city gates. Next he raided the Zagros Mountains, where 23 tribes had united against him. Again he was successful, exacting from the enemy an

Poignant relic of Mesopotamian slavery, this tiny footprint of a child remains embedded in a clay slab dating from about 1200 BC. The cuneiform inscription and other marks on the clay indicate that a husband and wife were forced to sell their children to a soothsayer named Bal Malik or themselves be enslaved for debt. The children were, however, too young to serve their master—who made the imprint of the boy's foot as proof of possession.

annual tribute of 2,000 head of cattle and 12,000 horses, vitally needed to pull the Assyrian war chariots. Finally, Tiglath-Pileser launched some 28 expeditions against the Arameans, on one occasion pushing on as far as the Mediterranean Sea. There he arranged trade agreements with the coastal city-states before making a triumphal visit to Egypt as a guest of the pharaoh of the day, who presented him with a live crocodile and arranged for him to hunt the *nahiru,* or "sea-horse," probably a dolphin.

It was a well-chosen diversion, for hunting appears to have been Tiglath-Pileser's chief pleasure. One text from the period tells of Tiglath-Pileser dispatching no fewer than 920 lions, 800 of them from his chariot and 120 on foot, as well as 10 elephants and six wild oxen, formidable creatures that stood six feet high at the shoulder. Such high numbers indicate that this was a controlled form of blood sport in which the animals, trapped in the wild, were released into some sort of game park for the benefit of their royal executioner. The fact that both elephants and wild oxen became extinct in Mesopotamia in ancient times may be linked to the excessive hunting appetites of Assyrian kings.

Tiglath-Pileser's immediate successors were not the mighty warriors that he had been, however, and the millennium came to a close in northern Mesopotamia on a quiet note, with a dearth of inscriptions suggesting a lack of events judged worthy enough to record. The gap was merely temporary. For before long, conqueror-kings of the Neo-Assyrian empire would follow in Tiglath-Pileser's mighty footsteps, spreading devastation and terror in their paths.

A BRUTAL VICTORY

The image above—Assyrian spearmen impaling Judean captives on stakes—was intended to inspire fear as well as awe in those who beheld it. But it was only one of several similar scenes that formed a chilling running narrative in the ceremonial chamber of the Southwest Palace at Nineveh.

There, guarded by a phalanx of colossal, winged stone bulls with human faces, this revealing, panoramic work stretched some 90 feet around the four walls and depicted key moments in the conquest of the Judean stronghold of Lachish by the Assyrian king Sennacherib in 701 BC.

Considered second only to Jerusalem in power in the eastern Mediterranean region, the walled citadel represented a linchpin in the Assyrian bid for control of the kingdom of Judah. "I besieged and conquered by stamping down earthramps and then by bringing up battering rams, by the assault of foot soldiers," boasted Sennacherib. His claim is echoed in the Old Testament,

which records that the sovereign "himself laid siege against Lachish, and all his power with him."

Eloquent testimony of this conflict lies in the long-buried fortress of Lachish, first excavated during the 1930s by British archaeologist James Leslie Starkey and more recently by Tel Aviv University's David Ussishkin. There, the charred, weapon-strewn ruins of a massive wall complex surrounding a palace fort, residential quarter, and commercial center have come to light. On the city's southwest corner, not far from the main gate, repose the remains of Sennacherib's siege ramp—thousands of tons of stone heaped to form a runway for mobile Assyrian battering rams that breached the upper portion of the walls. And as further evidence of the violence—and the success—of the Assyrian attack, shattered fragments of the bronze door fittings recall the moment when Sennacherib's troops finally smashed the citadel's gate and poured inside to bring down destruction on the population.

Assyrian infantrymen march two abreast through a stony landscape planted with grapevines and olive trees toward the citadel of Lachish, as shown in the above drawing of a segment of Sennacherib's palace reliefs (detail, right). At the fore stride the archers, bows at the ready. Slingers, stones cupped in their whirling leather slingshots, bring up the rear. Distinctive uniforms and hair styles suggest the ethnic diversity of the army, which routinely conscripted its conquered foes.

Deadly missiles, hundreds of arrowheads (above), and slingstones (right) littered Lachish. Diggers unearthed the heaviest concentration of arrowheads—leaf-shaped blades of iron or bone—near the city wall. Many were bent, indicating they had been shot at close range. Less plentiful but no less lethal were the slingstones, half-pound orbs of flint the size of tennis balls. Like arrowheads, they were launched by besiegers and defenders alike.

ATTACKING WITH BATTERING RAMS

Menaced by a hail of torches, arrows, and slingstones, Sennacherib's forces fight their way up the siege ramp toward Lachish's gatehouse (left) in the central panel of the relief. One of the Assyrian siege engines (far left)—wheeled assault towers equipped with metal-headed battering rams—leads the way. Attempts to set the leather and wood contraption ablaze are foiled by the engine's crew, who douse it with water using long-handled dippers (closeup, right). In compressing the action, the sculptor shows Judean deportees streaming from the gatehouse in the aftermath of the siege.

A vertical cross section cut through the Assyrian siege ramp looms like a dark scar at the southwest corner of Lachish (right). Above the ramp, sandbags mark off neat excavation pits beside the city wall, which rings the site a third of the way down the summit. The siege ramp apparently stopped just short of the wall, the reach of the battering rams being sufficient to bridge the gap.

THE CONSEQUENCES OF DEFIANCE

Among the Assyrian accouterments discovered in the rubble blanketing the siege ramp and city wall were a single bronze crest (above) and numerous bits of bronze or iron scale armor (above, right). The crest probably adorned the helmet of an Assyrian spearman, as seen below (third from left).

"Sennacherib, king of all, king of Assyria, sitting on his throne while the spoils from the city of Lachish passed before him," reads an inscription on the relief at right. Thus ensconced, the supreme commander is believed to have directed the battle—and celebrated the victory—from his camp just opposite the siege ramp. Later   perhaps after his murder by his sons—the king's features were defaced.

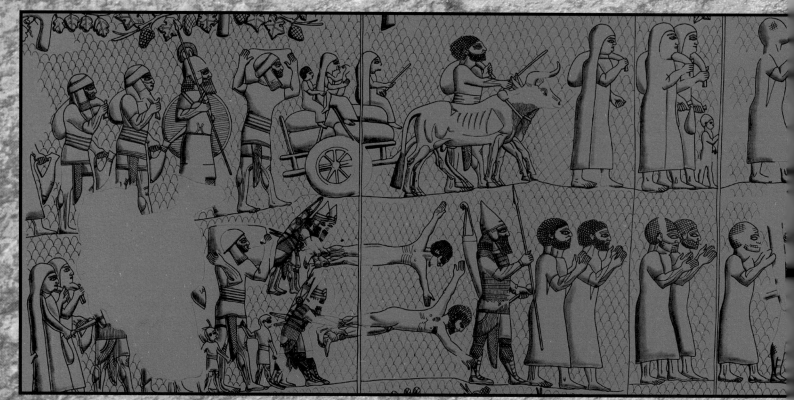

Under Assyrian guard, Judean captives file out of the vanquished city (above) toward a triumphant Sennacherib, who sits in judgment on his throne (far right). In

the upper column, two women, a child, and a babe in arms ride atop a bullock cart pulled by two malnourished oxen, while a barefoot man keeps pace alongside. Below, a

band of prisoners raise their hands in a plea for mercy as two captives (behind)— probably Judean officials—are flayed alive and another (in front) is stabbed to death.

ASSYRIA: AN EMPIRE BUILT ON BLOOD AND TRIBUTE

Delicate granulated goldwork frames an exquisite palm tree mosaic of semi-precious stones set in lapis lazuli. Perhaps symbolizing the Sacred Tree often depicted in Assyrian art, this eighth-century-BC pendant was found in 1989 in a queens' tomb at Nimrud, in Iraq.

Wielding brush and trowel, workers in April 1989 were removing the dirt of centuries from a buried palace at Nimrud, which had served as chief fortress and capital of the Assyrian empire from about 879 to 706 BC, when they noticed a fragment of ceramic piping. To their surprise, it turned out to be an air vent. This could mean only one thing—that the surface they were working on, previously assumed to be part of the palace floor, was actually a roof. Probing further, they found a tomb whose small antechamber led through two stone doors that pivoted on stone hinges into the main room. The closed sarcophagus within, made of a single piece of local stone covered with three slabs, had lain there apparently undisturbed since the day of its sealing.

The ancient sepulcher came equipped with a potent curse: "If anyone lays hands on my tomb," warned the Assyrian princess Yabaya, for whom the tomb had been constructed, "let the ghost of insomnia take hold of him for ever and ever." But by the time this message, inscribed in cuneiform upon a marble slab, was noticed, the 2,700-year-old burial chamber near the banks of the river Tigris had already been entered by Iraqi archaeologist Muzahim Mahmoud Hussein. The record does not indicate whether he lost any sleep over the matter, but if he did, it would have been from sheer excitement.

With an iron bar, Muzahim pried off the lid and saw something glinting through the dust. "When I held up the light," he reported, "it was reflected back into my eyes by the gold." And gold there was, in prodigious quantities, crafted into jewelry of astounding artistry, sparkling in and around two desiccated female skeletons, one much smaller than the other and therefore thought to be that of a child. Besides jewelry, there were scores of tiny, multipetaled, golden rosettes that some mourner's hand apparently had showered over the bodies of the departed before the sarcophagus was closed. Dazzled by the sight, Muzahim and his colleagues counted some 80 delicately wrought golden trinkets, weighing a total of about 31 pounds. Among the many artifacts were much older cylinder seals *(pages 23-25)* of the 14th and 13th centuries BC, which, in the eighth century BC, had been mounted in gold and worn as jewelry. Unidentified charred bones were found in a nearby gray stone vase.

What fascinated the archaeologists further were the inscriptions on four vessels of gold, and one of rock crystal, revealing the names of three queens, until then unknown to scholars: Yabaya, wife of Tiglath-Pileser III; Banitu, wife of Shalmaneser V; and Talya, wife of Sargon II. Their husbands ruled in succession from 744 to 705 BC, and the artifacts commemorating their wives confirmed for archaeologists that the palace had been used for nearly two centuries after the death of its principal builder, King Ashurnasirpal II, who reigned from 883 to 859 BC.

Yet another tomb was discovered four months later, holding even greater treasure. It is believed to be the tomb of Queen Mulisu, wife of Ashurnasirpal II, but the great stone coffin that dominated the chamber proved to be empty, and archaeologists believe her body may have been transferred elsewhere. The burial chamber also yielded three bronze coffins, each containing unidentified skeletons, and the room itself was crammed with items similar to the pieces previously encountered. The 440 golden artifacts, weighing, all told, about 51 pounds, included an extraordinary crown—fashioned like a miniature grape arbor and decorated with vines, grapes of lapis lazuli, and nude winged goddesses—and a vase only about five inches high, depicting in minute detail scenes of war and the hunt.

The government of Iraq, still smarting from a long war with Iran, was not rushing to trumpet the news and play host to a stream of foreign journalists and archaeologists. But word gradually spread, and many specialists in the field shared the excitement of the British Museum's John Curtis, who saw the finds and described them as "the most significant archaeological discovery since King Tut-ankhamen's tomb." As remarkable in its way as the discovery was that it had taken place on ground that had been zealously and repeatedly excavated by generations of archaeologists.

Now scholars had gained entry to the labyrinth of funeral cellars dug under the floors of the harem, in a time-honored Mesopotamian tradition. Above the complex of burial vaults, the consorts and concubines of Assyrian monarchs were housed in a series of rooms separated from the throne room and other royal reception rooms by an extremely thick wall.

The discovery of the tombs would prove immensely valuable to archaeologists. For one thing, little Assyrian gold survived the sack of Assyria's cities after the fall of the empire between 612 and 605 BC, and here suddenly was a rich cache to study. Moreover, the exquisite objects shed new light on Assyrian kings of the first millennium BC, who had been seen by modern scholars only as ruthless, highly successful warriors and imperialists. But these finds suggested that royal Assyrians possessed not just prodigious wealth but a keen eye for beauty and sophisticated craftsmanship as well.

Before the world's Assyriologists and journalists could pack their bags and head for Nimrud, however, Iraqi authorities, threatened by terrorists from disgruntled ethnic groups within its borders, discouraged the foreign press from visiting the area. Then in 1991, Muzahim's hopes of pursuing the hunt for the tombs of the Assyrian kings themselves were thwarted by the outbreak of the Gulf War.

Such military exigencies as these would have been well understood by the soldier-kings of the Neo-Assyrian era. Theirs was a culture of conquest. From 911 BC, when Assyrian armies marched westward out of Mesopotamia to settle old scores and restore the empire that had been lost by their ancestors some 200 years earlier, until they were undone by a coalition of enemies in the late seventh century BC, northern Mesopotamian monarchs would dominate much of the Middle East. In these, its days of glory, Assyria would hold sway over the lands running from Egypt to the Zagros Mountains in Iran. Its kings imposed their will upon countless tribes, city-states, and nations, caused a golden river of tribute and treasure to flow into their coffers, and moved entire populations to satisfy their imperial ends.

Nearly every record of that age and region—whether written

ARCHAEOLOGICAL PRIZES
OF RARE DELIGHT

As Iraqi archaeologists lifted off the stone lid of a sarcophagus at Nimrud in 1989, they beheld the remains of two females, a young woman and a girl. The skeletons were covered with gold: crowns, rings, earrings, and bracelets, many embedded with carnelian, agate, lapis lazuli, and turquoise. Nearby, more jewelry and vases of bronze, alabaster, and crystal were piled high. Bowls, cups, and flasks, also of gold, lay on the skeletons or under the skulls. Among the bones were tiny gold rosettes *(backdrop)*, once dress ornaments.

Commenting on the craftsmanship of these exquisite artifacts, British archaeologist Georgina Herrman noted that "it sets a magnificent standard. The workmanship would be difficult to duplicate today."

A masterpiece of the jeweler's art, the granulated gold pendant above is set with semiprecious stones. The gold necklace (below, left), heavy with 28 pendants, fastens with a clasp of intertwined animal heads. Among the 72 sets of gold earrings found in the tomb with these pieces, one pair (below) is formed by cones dangling from half-moons.

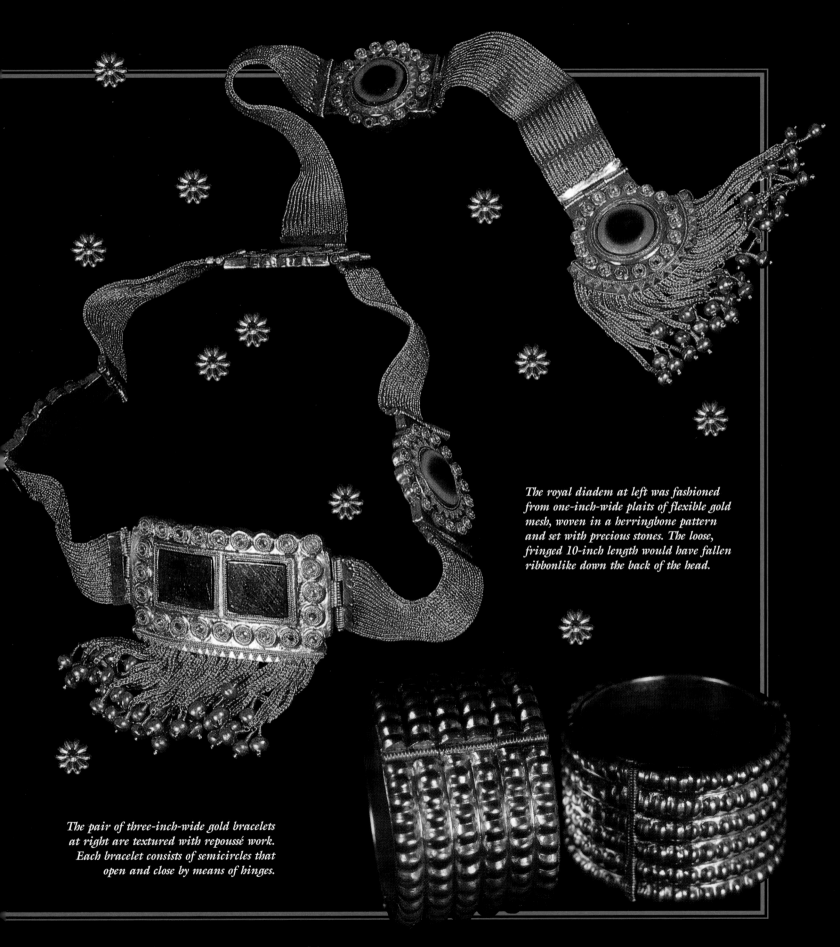

The royal diadem at left was fashioned from one-inch-wide plaits of flexible gold mesh, woven in a herringbone pattern and set with precious stones. The loose, fringed 10-inch length would have fallen ribbonlike down the back of the head.

The pair of three-inch-wide gold bracelets at right are textured with repoussé work. Each bracelet consists of semicircles that open and close by means of hinges.

The 3½-inch-wide gold crown at right, appliquéd with three rows of rosettes, may have been worn by the child buried with the queen. Below, a pair of heavy gold bracelets reveals inlays of tiger's-eye, turquoise, malachite, and lapis lazuli.

Above, a delicate gold chain adorns a miniature flute vase, about three inches high. An exquisite wide-mouthed golden bowl (left), about 10 inches in diameter, is embellished with rows of raised nodes.

in hieroglyphics upon the walls of an Egyptian pharaoh's tomb or inscribed upon parchment scrolls preserving the sacred memories of the Jews—bears some mark of the Assyrian presence. And Assyria's own cuneiform chronicles confirm the truth of these encounters.

Unlike their Egyptian contemporaries, however, the Assyrians of the first millennium BC seemed, for a long time, to have vanished from history almost without trace. Then, in the 19th century AD, dramatic monuments, such as the massive human-headed bulls of Nimrud, set the West agog when, after epic journeys, they reached Europe's great museums *(pages 112-121)*. Excavated palaces revealed a rich legacy: walls lined with meticulously detailed, pictorial chronicles of armies on the march, sieges and executions, royal lion hunts, and processions of exotically costumed foreigners delivering tribute to Assyria's sovereigns.

The saga of Assyria's rediscovery by the modern world began in the early 1840s, when traders in the bazaars of the old Mesopotamian city of Mosul, on the upper Tigris 220 miles northwest of Baghdad, observed a handsome, dark-haired European obsessively sifting through the heaped-up curios for sale on their stalls. Anything that looked sufficiently venerable could arouse his intense interest. In excellent Arabic he bargained, agreed upon a price, clutched the cracked pot or inscribed brick, and then interrogated the vendors as to where they had found the objects. The traders simply remarked that such things were everywhere. Indeed, in the rural districts they practically sprouted from the ground.

When not haggling in Mosul's bazaars, Paul Emile Botta served as the French consul in this remote outpost of the Ottoman Empire whose Turkish sultans had ruled the region since the 16th century. Botta was a brilliant linguist, a world traveler with a passion for the landscape and antiquities of the Middle East. His superiors in the French government had seen a way to put this knowledge to use in the service of his country. They were eager to stake a Gallic claim to the ancient treasures now believed to await discovery in the Mesopotamian earth and were well aware that their European neighbors were equally keen to embellish their own national museums with such finds. So they had encouraged Botta to pursue his antiquarian enthusiasms among the promising mounds on the Tigris's banks.

Botta had little luck with his first attempts at excavation. One likely looking mound stood uncomfortably close to an Islamic shrine, and the local clergy reacted with fury to the threat of desecration.

Turning to a second hillock at Kuyunjik, just across the Tigris from Mosul, which Botta believed to be the site of Nineveh, the Assyrian city of biblical fame, the Frenchman toiled for several months and brought forth no more than some bricks and bits of alabaster. The disappointed consul found it hard to muster enthusiasm for another potentially fruitless dig when, in March 1843, a peasant from the village of Khorsabad, 12 miles northeast of Kuyunjik, appeared at his door with a load of inscribed bricks for sale and a tale of the rich archaeological pickings in his own home district. It sounded too good to be true, and Botta half-heartedly dispatched a pair of workmen to investigate the site.

A week later, Botta joyfully saddled his horse and rode hard for Khorsabad, for word had come back of richly carved limestone walls, bearing the images of bearded men and monstrous beasts, exposed almost at the first touch of the workmen's spades. Botta immediately recognized these figures as the work of a hitherto unknown civilization, apparently as ancient as the Egyptian but completely alien to it in form. "I believe myself to be the first who has discovered sculptures which with some reason can be referred to the period when Nineveh was flourishing," he wrote excitedly in a report to Paris.

Until now the map of the known ancient world had contained little more than Egypt, Greece, Rome, and the lands of the Jews, Israel and Judah. From biblical references Assyria was understood to have been a major force in its day, but there was no physical evidence of its existence. Botta could feel the breath of other eager explorers on his neck. So too could the French government. They dispatched funds for further excavation and also sent Botta an extremely useful colleague, Eugene Napoleon Flandin, an artist skilled in the portrayal of ancient ruins and monuments, bearing a commission to record every detail of Botta's finds.

Bureaucratic wrangles with the Ottoman government took time and energy, especially when a corrupt local official, Mohammed Keritli Oglu, pasha of Mosul, played cat and mouse, teasing Botta by first giving, and then rescinding, permission to occupy and excavate the sites. When Botta was finally allowed to dig, the pasha sent spies to ensure that the French consul did not make off with whatever treasure appeared. Local laborers were quietly warned that if they failed to pass on a share of any gold found to the pasha himself, they would be tortured. With this threat in mind, many peasants chose in-them in a building especially designed in the Assyrian style. His home, Canford Manor, was eventually converted into a school, and the last of his ancient prizes was presumably sold off in 1959. The Assyrian building became the school's candy store and the relief an unintended target of errant darts thrown by the boys.

The cleaned work depicts two figures. To the right is a eunuch carrying a mace, a bow, and a quiver and wearing rosette wristbands that show his royal affiliation. Following is a winged divinity holding a pine cone, an age-old symbol meant to provide magical protection.

Once dismissed as a worthless plaster cast, the relief sold at a London auction in 1994 for a world-record price of £7.7 million, or $11.9 million.

stead to abandon their new employer and stick to the safer course of tilling their own fields. Botta called the pasha "a little Nero," and sought new workers from among a group of Christians who had recently settled in the district and were only too glad of any means of making a living.

Such obstacles as these, however, were overshadowed by the magnificence and profusion of the discoveries made during the summer of 1844. Day by day, Botta's workmen penetrated the buried remains of a royal palace. Massive sculptures of fantastic creatures—lions and bulls with the wings of mythical monsters and the heads of human beings—stood guard at its gates and portals. Within were the glorious walls of corridors, audience chambers, temples, and treasuries, many decorated with bas-relief images of warfare, hunting parties, state ceremonies, and religious rites.

Those surfaces not covered with sculpted pictures bore blocks of explanatory text, inscribed—to Botta's frustration—in the mysterious cuneiform symbols that would not be deciphered for some years to come. Only then would its discoverer learn that this palace was a royal fortress named Dur Sharrukin, erected to the specifications of the eighth-century-BC Assyrian monarch Sargon II.

In the autumn of 1844, the artist Flandin returned to France, bearing in triumph his drawings of the Khorsabad finds. Scholars and ordinary citizens alike were dazzled by what they saw. A fever of Assyriomania gripped the French capital, and the government ordered Botta to send home the finest of these marvelous sculptures for exhibition at the Louvre *(pages 120-121)*.

The British, vying with the French for influence in the region, looked on with envy. If more archaeological wonders were about to emerge from Mesopotamian soil and ancient history to be rewritten by these discoveries, then Great Britain wanted its share of the loot and acclaim.

"It pains me grievously," wrote Henry Rawlinson, British emissary to Baghdad and himself a pioneer in the study of Mesopotamian antiquities, to his colleague, Stratford Canning, ambassador to Constantinople, "to see the French monopolize the field." Botta's celebrated finds, Rawlinson predicted, would "constitute a national glory in future ages, when perhaps the Turkish Empire that we are now struggling so hard to preserve shall be but a matter of history."

Canning agreed, and he knew just the person to pursue British interests in this area. His choice was Austen Henry Layard, who had traveled extensively through the Middle East before joining Canning's staff in Constantinople as a specialist in Mesopotamian and Persian affairs. "Such a nice fellow," was how a compatriot described Layard, "very clever and very amusing." A young man of many talents, Layard had struck up a friendship with Botta on the grounds of their shared passion for archaeology and their belief that the region's hidden mysteries were about to be laid bare.

With instructions from Canning to keep a low profile and to avoid all entanglements in local political and religious disputes, Layard was duly dispatched in October 1845 to Mosul. Announcing loudly that he had come to the district to hunt wild boar, Layard and a friend from the British consulate loaded a raft with everything needed for the chase, including greyhounds. Underneath the conspicuous bundles of spears and guns were tucked parcels of tools for excavation. The party floated for seven hours down the Tigris to a group of tantalizing mounds set on a bluff some two miles beyond the river's northeast bank, 20 miles from Mosul.

On the morning of November 9, 1845, with half a dozen laborers recruited by a friendly local sheik, Layard set to work, digging exploratory trenches. Within a matter of hours, they had discovered not one but two Assyrian palaces, later identified by deciphered inscriptions as the royal residence of Ashurnasirpal II in the ninth century BC and as a never completed edifice begun some 200 years later by a successor named Esarhaddon.

Layard, however, did not know what he was excavating. He believed he was digging in Nineveh, where the biblical prophet Jonah had allegedly preached, and he thought Nineveh was the name, not of a city, but of a country. In fact he had found Nimrud, a city called Calah in the Bible, and sometime capital of Assyria. He was ecstatic at the caches of beautiful ivory carvings, bricks inscribed with

ESSAI DE RESTAURATION

Stone colossi guard one of the seven double-towered gateways to Sargon II's palace at Khorsabad as rendered in a 19th-century reconstruction by artist Felix Thomas, who accompanied French archaeologist Victor Place on the excavation. Glazed bricks ornamented the arches.

cuneiform texts, and sculpted tablets bearing vibrant battle scenes of chariot warfare and a city under siege. In a letter home to a devoted aunt, he declared, "I live among the ruins and dream of little else."

But his joy at these discoveries, and those unearthed in the weeks that followed, was soon to be dampened. Botta's adversary, the pasha of Mosul, was up to his old tricks. One day he sent word that no further excavation would be permitted. Mounting a horse, Layard rode hard for Mosul. Within a few hours he was face to face with the pasha, who greeted him with the greatest amiability and assured him that he was perfectly delighted for Layard to continue his explorations. But no sooner had the Englishman returned to his dig when another messenger fetched him back to Mosul.

The pasha, with furrowed brow, announced to "dear Mr. Layard" that he was fearful for the man's physical safety. The mounds Layard was excavating were Muslim burial places, and he could not guarantee his esteemed guest's safety if they were disturbed. "Your

The vividly decorated throne room of Ashurnasirpal II at Nimrud displays paintings and wall sculptures of kings, priests, genies, warriors, and charioteers in a reconstruction published in the 1850s by Austen Henry Layard. Nimrud, known as the ancient city of Calah in the Bible, was founded by Ashurnasirpal as his administrative capital in 879 BC.

life is more valuable than old stones," the wily pasha reminded him. Layard was puzzled; in weeks of digging he had seen no gravestones. Two days of arguing with the pasha did no good, and Layard rode back to his excavation site to find that an entire cemetery-full of burials had somehow miraculously appeared on ground that had been empty 50 hours before.

One of the pasha's own men, Captain Daud, confessed that his soldiers had been ordered to perpetrate the sham. They had spent grueling hours moving a burial ground, marker by marker, at ridiculous speed. "We have killed our horses and ourselves in carrying these accursed stones!" he exclaimed.

The truth behind the trickery emerged: The pasha's sabotage had been at the behest of the French consul, who did not want Great Britain muscling in on France's quest for archaeological supremacy in Iraq. A bribe from Layard soon eased the captain's aching back, and the dig continued, finally gaining the official blessing of Ottoman officials, who issued permission for the export of sculptures and other finds.

The hunt for monumental treasures, rather than a detailed investigation of the site itself, was Layard's first priority. His success was spectacular: Out of the earth came 13 pairs of lions with wings, a

Among the very few three-dimensional Assyrian stone statues to survive, this half-size portrait of Ashurnasirpal II once stood in the shrine of Ishtar at Nimrud. The bare-headed king, draped in the fringed shawl that was the court dress of Assyria, reflects the imposing and unrelenting image of Assyrian rulers.

mighty winged bull with the bearded head of a human king, a collection of elegant alabaster vases, and pieces of military equipment, ranging from armor to helmets like those worn by the sculpted soldiers in the bas-reliefs.

After one particular trench was thought to have yielded up all its secrets, the workmen came upon one of the most dramatic discoveries of the day: A nearly seven-foot-tall Black Obelisk *(page 95),* carved with cuneiform text and 20 bas-reliefs, portrayed in scrupulous detail the ceremonial presentation of tribute sent by foreign kings as a mark of deference to an Assyrian monarch. The drama depicted turned out to have a strong biblical connection, for one tribute giver was the ninth-century-BC Israelite king Jehu, who had wiped out the house of King Ahab and had broken faith with his allies in the neighboring kingdom of Judah. To purchase the friendship of the region's great power, he duly delivered gold, silver, and other tokens of deference to the Assyrian king Shalmaneser III.

The Black Obelisk, after a journey as perilous as that undertaken by Botta's treasures a few years earlier, rose anew in the Assyrian gallery at the British Museum. Layard's heroic efforts to retrieve these artifacts, however, reaped little gratitude from the home office. Instead he was subject to a set of patronizing instructions for the care of sculptures in transit. Layard remarked, with some justification, that he had been "treated like a master-bricklayer" by pundits who had never journeyed much beyond the stately exhibition halls in London's Bloomsbury.

Believing that he had been excavating in the biblical Nineveh, Layard produced a lavishly illustrated account of his discoveries, entitled *Nineveh and Its Remains.* Despite this error in naming the site, Layard's book provided a mine of archaeological information, impressing both skeptical scholars and a great mass of ordinary readers, who were enthralled by the emergence of a rich civilization with biblical associations. "The most extraordinary work of the present age," was the verdict of the *London Times* reviewer, shortly after the book's publication in the winter of 1849. The surge of public interest helped shame the guardians of the purse at the British Museum to increase their less-than-generous subsidies for Layard's endeavors.

The actual city of Nineveh, in time identified by cuneiform inscriptions, would also be explored by Layard, beginning in 1847. Its site included the set of mounds at Kuyunjik that Botta had been certain was the legendary city and had probed at the beginning of his archaeological career without much success. Botta's problem was that he had not been able to reach Nineveh's buildings, buried some 20 feet below ground, a depth to which Layard was prepared to sink his trench. In 1849 Layard exposed the Southwest Palace built by Sennacherib, who ruled from 704 to 681 BC. He excavated 71 of the structure's rooms and found some 2,000 sculptured slabs. For scholars now homing in on the secrets of cuneiform script, however, Layard's most thrilling discovery at Nineveh was a section of the imperial library, in the great Northwest Palace of Sennacherib's grandson Ashurbanipal, built in the mid seventh century BC and crammed with detailed records, treaties, and chronicles of Assyrian history. With its additional collections of bilingual vocabularies, as well as works of literature, medicine, ritual, astronomy, and mathematics, the library laid the foundation for a comprehensive grasp of Assyrian culture.

Even such triumphs as these, however, could not compensate for Layard's distress at the paltry sums provided by the British Museum for his work. He complained repeatedly that he had been forced to subsidize digs out of his own far-from-bottomless resources. Finally, in 1851, in poor health, he despaired of receiving adequate funds, quit his excavation, leaving his assistant Hormuzd Rassam in charge of further excavation, and left Mosul.

As Layard journeyed downriver, looking out upon a landscape that still held so many secrets, he may well have remembered a question posed to him by his friend Sheik Abd-ur-rahman, during a feast he gave at Nimrud, "In the name of the Most High, tell me, O Bey, what are you going to do with those stones? So many thousands of purses spent upon such things!" Perhaps Layard might have concluded that the sheik had aptly summed up his compatriots when he went on to say, "These figures will not teach you to make any better knives, or scissors, or chintzes; and it is in the making of those things that the English show their wisdom."

The English, however, soon proved wise in another way. Four years after Layard left field archaeology in Mesopotamia, Britain's Royal Asiatic Society set up an experiment to prove that the handful of scholars who had been laboring for more than half a century at the complex task of decipherment now held the key to cuneiform within their grasp. The society asked four students of the field, including Layard's colleague, Henry Rawlinson, former consul general at Baghdad, to attempt separate translations of a single, newly discovered cuneiform text. In 1857 the four versions were scrutinized, and the society was delighted to announce that all four individuals had arrived at more or less the same interpretation. The British Museum now set several copyists to work on the cuneiform tablets within its possession, to prepare published versions of these texts for eventual translation.

The decipherment of cuneiform solved archaeological and historical mysteries that would have been beyond the capabilities of Botta or Layard. Armed with this knowledge and with superior technical expertise, 20th-century investigators, such as Britain's Professor Max Mallowan, returned to the sites first opened by these pioneers.

Mallowan had two priorities when he

From his chariot, King Ashurnasirpal II takes aim at an attacking lion in this carved alabaster relief found at Nimrud's Northwest Palace. Organized lion hunts, in which the caged beasts were released within an enclosure formed by armed soldiers holding interlocking shields, gave the king a chance to practice his hunting skills with little risk to life and limb. They also provided an exciting diversion in the intervals between military campaigns.

arrived at Nimrud in 1949 accompanied by his wife, mystery writer Agatha Christie. He hoped to find more of the magnificent carved ivories first unearthed by Layard, and he believed that, somewhere within the ruins, he would discover the archives of the royal capital.

"It seemed incredible to me," Mallowan declared in his memoirs, "that so large a city could have been devoid of economic, business, historical and literary texts. I would have staked my life that in the end we would find all these things, and find them we did."

With a small staff and 70 hired villagers, Mallowan set to work at one of the sites first opened by Layard at Nimrud, the elaborate structure known as the Northwest Palace, built in the ninth century BC by Ashurnasirpal II. But what Layard had identified as the palace was merely a small segment of a much larger complex of courtyards, treasure chambers, administrative blocks, and domestic quarters. Almost as soon as the work began, Mallowan came upon a delicately carved ivory cow, small enough to hold in the palm of his hand, lying on a surviving fragment of palace floor.

It was an auspicious beginning. As the excavation proceeded, prodigious quantities of magnificently sculpted ivory emerged (*pages 98-99*). Gingerly excavating a deep well, for example, the team came upon a pair of ivory plaques, decorated with gold leaf, inlaid carnelian, and lapis lazuli, displaying similar scenes of violent death in a lush landscape, in which a man writhes in the clutches of a lion. A wealth of other remarkably ornate carvings included two that were shaped into the likenesses of women's heads. The team dubbed one beauty Mona Lisa, while the second sculpture, of a less attractive woman, became the Ugly Sister. Identifying these objects as broken-off pieces of ivory furniture, Mallowan wondered what circumstances had brought them to the bottom of a well, and he suspected they had been flung there by enemy invaders sacking the palace during the empire's last days.

Preserving these fragile objects once they had made contact with the air posed a challenge. Their color and texture altered rapidly, shifting from a pale yellow hue and a soft, almost cheeselike consistency to a white brittleness. The team tried out various protective techniques to keep the ivories from crumbling to dust. Expedition member Joan Oates recalled that the most effective solution came from Agatha Christie, who, when not working on her latest crime novel, helped with the day-to-day running of the excavation. Christie suggested to her husband that he try coating the ivories with the

The exploits of King Shalmaneser III and scenes of tribute bearers leading an elephant, a rhinoceros, a camel, a lion, and a stag are carved in bas-relief on this 6½-foot-tall, ziggurat-topped monument. Excavated by Austen Henry Layard at Nimrud in 1846, the Black Obelisk pictures Shalmaneser receiving tribute from Jehu, ruler of Israel.

hand cream she had brought along to protect her fair English skin from the Mesopotamian sun. Mallowan took her advice, and the treatment became standard practice on the dig.

As he continued his investigation of Nimrud's important structures, Mallowan came upon the second great object of his quest, a library of cuneiform tablets recording affairs of state, history, financial transactions, treaties, and other subjects of importance to the Assyrian court. Fittingly, the discovery was made in the Nabu Temple, a shrine dedicated to the god of writing. Here, Mallowan also found a document naming the various sections of the temple itself, providing him with the rare opportunity of employing the building's original occupants as his guides to the site. This text, however, could not have led Mallowan to the incomparable treasures discovered by Muzahim in 1988-1989, even though much of the time he was excavating at Nimrud, he was walking over the royal tombs that would have been his greatest discoveries.

The work of Mallowan and his successors at Nimrud shed fresh light on the era when Assyria resumed its place as the great central power of a turbulent Middle East. The final decade of the 10th century BC, and the first quarter of the century that followed, had witnessed the success of the Assyrian king Adad-Nirari II and his heirs in protecting their once mighty homeland from invading nomadic tribes who had encroached upon it. Although neighboring peoples had deprived Assyria of its former colonies and had strangled trade routes, its kings nonetheless were able to retain the heartland between the rivers.

Self-defense, however, involved more than simply hanging on to a shrinking turf. It meant turning enemy kings into cowed vassals, while economic self-interest demanded subdued territories that would pay tribute or be easily plundered. And if divine aid was to be sought, then devotion to Assur, god above all other gods, dictated the spread of his cult as far as Assyria's sword could reach. All these motives required a centralized, controlling power.

The great edifices that modern archaeologists would uncover at Nimrud attest to the success of Assyrian endeavors. King Ashurnasirpal II, who reigned from 883 to 859 BC, desired to mark his greatness by building a new capital at Nimrud, well away from the more vulnerable city of Assur, with its ancient memories, ghosts, and relics of dead kings. Thousands of workers toiled on the five miles of enclosing walls, the canal that would bring water to the town and fields nearby, and the acropolis with its temples, towering ziggurat, and royal residence.

By 879 BC the city rose, sparkling above the plain, and Ashurnasirpal stood back to contemplate his achievement with some pride. A lengthy inscription, carved on a block of sandstone at the entrance to his throne room, was found in 1951 by excavators from the British School of Archaeology in Iraq. Upon it Ashurnasirpal announced to posterity that "the palace of cedar, cypress, juniper, boxwood, mulberry, pistachio wood and tamarisk, for my royal dwelling and for my lordly pleasure for all time, I founded therein. Beasts of the mountains and of the seas, of white limestone and alabaster I fashioned and set them up in its gates." The palace was also a storehouse of plunder, "Silver, gold, lead, copper, and iron, the spoil of my hand from the lands which I had brought under my sway, in great quantities I took and placed therein."

To make certain that his accomplishments would not go unnoticed, the king reported, within the same inscription, that he had held a 10-day-long feast, inviting "47,074 persons, men and women, who were bid to come from across my entire country," plus another 5,000 foreign dignitaries, 1,500 court officials, and 16,000 of the local townspeople "from all ways of life." The menu is also recorded in meticulous and abundant detail. It featured meat, fish, and game, including 1,000 cattle, 1,000 calves, mutton and lamb in even greater quantity, ducks, geese, doves, and other birds of land and water num-

A stone carving of Ashurnasirpal's military camp shows food being prepared in the top left and two right-hand panels. In the lower left one, priests examine the entrails of a sacrificed animal to divine the future.

bering some 33,000, and 1,000 stags and gazelles. These delicacies were accompanied by bread, onions, greens, pickled and spiced fruit, eggs, and seeds; washed down with veritable lakes of beer and wine; and followed by cheese, nuts, honey, pomegranates, grapes, and an orchard's worth of fruits not yet identified by the inscription's translators.

Ashurnasirpal may have played the role of a smiling host for the 10 days of the party, but in the lands he had plundered for the wealth to build Nimrud, he inspired only horror. For he was a conqueror whose cruelty, even in an age not known for its mild-mannered kings, was considerable. On an inscription, for example, the king reports, with some degree of professional pride: "Many of the captives taken I burned in a fire. Many I took alive; from some I cut off their hands to the wrist, from others I cut off their noses, ears and fingers; I put out the eyes of many of the soldiers. I burnt their young men and women to death." In another vanquished city, according to his own account, Ashurnasirpal taught a salutary lesson to those refusing to yield to his greater power. He stacked up the corpses from the battle in front of the town gates, claiming "I flayed the nobles, as many as had rebelled, and spread their skins out on the piles."

These shock tactics brought success, for in 877 BC, after an inexorable march across the Euphrates at Carchemish, traversing the plain of Antioch, over the Orontes River, and into the shadow of Mount Lebanon, an elated Ashurnasirpal announced his arrival upon the Mediterranean shore, "I cleaned my weapons in the deep sea and performed sheep-offerings to the gods." Assyria, once again, had triumphed.

This military machine rolled on under the command of Ashurnasirpal's son, Shalmaneser III, who succeeded to the throne in 858 BC. His ambition, it seemed, was to outdo his father. He spent 31 years of his 35-year reign waging war. After a clash near the river Orontes with Syrian foes from Hama and Damascus, he boasted, "I slew 14,000 of their warriors with the sword. I rained destruction upon them. The plain was too small to let their bodies fall; the wide countryside was used up in burying them. With their corpses, I spanned the Orontes as with a bridge."

97

WONDERS OF EXQUISITELY CARVED IVORY

Thousands of ivories dating from the eighth and ninth centuries BC have been recovered at Nimrud. Often the work of Phoenician or Syrian artisans, they were amassed by Assyrian kings as tribute or loot from their military campaigns. Many were originally covered with gold foil, encrusted with semiprecious stones, or stained with dyes, like the smiling face at right, called the Mona Lisa of Nimrud by the British excavators who found the piece in 1952.

The incomplete figure of the young hunter with painted yellow tresses and a white kilt at left once showed him struggling to spear a lion whose claws can still be seen on his arm and hip. At right, a lioness mauls a shepherd, one of a pair of furniture plaques. The victim's curls were rendered with tiny inserted pegs of gilt ivory.

A harpy with wings open (left) grips the carcass of a goat while vultures feed on either side. Below, a tribute bearer, carved in the round, leads an oryx while carrying a monkey on his left shoulder and a leopard skin over the right.

At Nimrud, Shalmaneser built a palace that far outshone Ashurnasirpal's architectural efforts. Nearly twice the size of its older neighbor, it covered an area of approximately 12 acres and comprised more than 200 rooms. In March 1957 Max Mallowan virtually stumbled upon the first sign of its presence while taking an off-duty stroll with one of his colleagues on the dig. They spotted a brick bearing an inscription and picked it up to discover that it was marked with the name Shalmaneser III. To the puzzlement at first of his companions, Mallowan began calling this sector of the site "F.S." The initials, he explained to them, stood for "Fort Shalmaneser."

Mallowan was, it seemed, prescient. For although Shalmaneser had called the place his royal palace, a successor, Esarhaddon, was more accurate in describing it as an arsenal. And Mallowan's excavation soon revealed the reason: Not only had this vast structure been a luxurious and imposing royal residence housing king, courtiers, clerks, women of the harem, and a hard-worked domestic staff, it had also been a base for the Assyrian army, a fortress behind a 300-yard barricade of mud-brick towers.

Within its perimeter, troops gathered up their armor and weapons to parade across broad, open courtyards, passing the brick reviewing stand where their commanders—and perhaps the king himself—stood ready to accept their salute. In off-duty hours these soldiers slept in barracks well supplied with washing facilities and

Two nearly symmetrical carved figures of Ashurnasirpal II face a stylized Sacred Tree and are flanked by benevolent genies. Raising a pine cone in the right hand and carrying a bucket in the left, each genie performs a divine ritual giving magical protection. In this stone relief from the Northwest Palace at Nimrud, the king, in his role as high priest, lifts his hand in worship to the winged disk overhead, where the god Assur resides.

woke to take their turns upon a huge crenelated tower, to watch for any enemies reckless enough to invade.

But the part of the structure that dominated the complex was the palace's massive throne room. Visible from a vast distance across the plain, it soared nearly 40 feet. Excavations of this enormous royal chamber suggested that Shalmaneser's tendency to outstrip his father extended as well to his interior decoration. For the room's lofty walls were lined with magnificent painted murals instead of the stone reliefs that adorned the smaller throne room of Ashurnasirpal.

When British archaeologist David Oates, who took over the direction of the excavation at Nimrud from 1958 to 1962, dug deep into the layers of rubble that choked the throne room, he discovered that, although the sovereign's chair itself had vanished, its base remained, a 15-ton stepped podium, decorated by carefully worked friezes depicting a royal ceremony. Upon it, an inscription proclaimed that this throne had been erected for Shalmaneser III, in the 13th year of his reign, or 845 BC.

Whatever the relations between Shalmaneser and his father, they could not have deteriorated as far as those between Shalmaneser and one of his sons. This prince not only rebelled against his father's long rule in 828 BC, but also persuaded 27 Assyrian cities, including Nineveh and Assur, to join the revolt. The now aged Shalmaneser sent out the rebel prince's younger brother, Shamshi-Adad, to quell the uprising; meanwhile, languishing in his palace, he received dispatches on the progress of the ensuing civil war. The turmoil, which pitted rural nobles and townspeople against the corrupt provincial governors and petty tyrants of the royal court, would last until three years after Shalmaneser's death in 824 BC and would usher in eight decades of political instability and economic decline, since Assyria's vassal-states saw no reason to continue sending tribute to a now toothless neighbor.

From this time of Assyrian obscurity, there nonetheless emerged a heroine, whose memory would survive for nearly three millennia, reach mythical status, and capture the imagination of Europe. The Assyrians knew her as their queen Sammuramat, called Semiramis in later traditions, royal daughter-in-law to the late Shalmaneser III, and wife to his son, now Shamshi-Adad V, who had been victorious in the civil war. In spite of the fact that, after her spouse's early death, she ruled as regent in the name of her infant son, Assyrian chroniclers give her little or no attention. It was left to

Greek writers, such as Ctesias, who served as physician to the king of Persia in the fifth century BC, to perpetuate her legend.

In these accounts Semiramis became more than human. Said to be the fierce Amazon offspring of a goddess, she was credited with founding great cities—or destroying them—and vanquishing half the major powers of the age, before turning into a dove at the moment of her death. Even when Assyria itself was forgotten, her name and legend survived: The 19th-century composer Rossini created an opera, *Semiramide*, to tell the story of a woman who may—or may not—have been, as one scholar put it, "the most beautiful, most cruel, most powerful and most lustful of Oriental queens."

Assyria's temporary decline allowed another regional power to flex its muscles. The adjoining kingdom of Urartu, occupying what today is eastern Turkey, northwestern Iran, and Armenia, was a prosperous realm, ruled by warrior-kings who had maintained a continuous readiness for war in response to the growing Assyrian threat. As Assyria's influence diminished, Urartu's expanded accordingly. But eventually Assyria gathered its resources and under King Tiglath-Pileser III, who ruled from 745 to 727 BC, began to fight back. This monarch vowed to "smash like pots" those smaller kingdoms that had allied themselves with Urartu. He was well-organized, efficient, and ruthless, and historians credit him with the transformation of Assyria from powerful kingdom to full-scale empire.

Tiglath-Pileser's military successes were achieved, in part, by establishing a permanent standing army to augment the traditional force of conscripts who returned home after battle to resume their civilian lives. He also enhanced the role of the cavalry. In the mountainous regions where wars against the Urartu and other foes were increasingly fought, a horse was far more flexible than a cumbersome war chariot, which could become bogged down or overturn.

As an aftermath to conquest, Tiglath-Pileser prepared the ground for Assyrian power in vanquished territories by mass deportations. Entire communities—men, women, and children by the thousands—were run out of their native places and escorted by Assyrian troops to new homes many hundreds of miles away. The king forced 30,000 Syrians, for instance, to walk from Hama, their home on the Orontes River in present-day Lebanon, to the Zagros Mountains, about 600 miles away. Some 154,000 southern Mesopotamians found themselves on the move in a single year. The practice, which would be enthusiastically continued by Tiglath-Pileser's successors,

was not simply a means of rubbing salt into the wounds of the vanquished. Tiglath-Pileser believed that these populations, wrenched from familiar ground and the haunts of their old gods, would more easily lose their particular tribal identities and evolve into tractable members of a new, expanded Assyrian empire.

Even those conquered peoples not uprooted and driven from plain to mountain, or vice versa, were deprived of their native rulers. These local kings and chieftains were replaced by governors sent out from the Assyrian capital; their realms became provinces of Assyria,

Chariots of Shalmaneser III, upper register, and the slaughter of the men of Hazau, lower register, are among the military narratives portrayed on sixteen 11-inch bronze bands that adorned temple gates at Balawat, the king's summer palace. The 21-foot-high wood doors were not hinged but were attached to vertical posts that turned on pivot stones. This curved section of the band wrapped around the post.

instead of foreign vassal-states. The king continued to demand hefty amounts of money from these regions, but the payments now counted not as foreign tribute but as domestic tax.

To create and perpetuate this new infrastructure, Tiglath-Pileser established an efficient system of communications, with messengers carrying communiques from the center to the new peripheral districts. Although his governors were permitted considerable legal and administrative power, a constant stream of royal directives ensured that these worthies remained firmly under the king's control. Information flowed both ways, especially in matters related to the defense of the realm. One individual, for example, who had provided useful intelligence on tribal activities in Babylonia, received a personal word of thanks from his ruler, "The man who loves the house of his lords opens the ears of his lords to whatever he sees or hears. It is good that you have sent a message."

The Urartian menace, however, did not disappear overnight. Only in the reign of Sargon II, who ruled from 722 to 705 BC, did Assyria alleviate this threat to her domination. And it was no easy task. Sargon II himself acknowledged that "As to the people who live in that area in the land of Urartu, their like does not exist for skill with cavalry horses." The mountainous regions where Urartu held sway made warfare doubly difficult. The army needed not only its own brave horsemen, but a corps of engineers as well to ensure some kind of passage over the peaks and precipices.

In a document cast in the form of a letter to "Assur, father of the gods, the gods and goddesses of Destiny, the city and its inhabitants, and the palace in its midst," Sargon II described the feats of his engineers during the Assyrian campaign of 714 BC in what today is Kurdistan. In true magisterial style, the ruler claimed most of the credit for their work: "With picks of bronze, I armed my pioneers. The crags of high mountains they caused to fly in splinters; they improved the passage. I took the head of my troops. The chariots, the cavalry, the fighters who went beside me, I made fly over this mountain like valiant eagles."

Sargon's wars against Urartu may have been successful in their short-term objectives, but neither he nor any later Assyrian king ever subjugated this independent and powerful kingdom, which continued to exist as long as did Assyria itself. By the seventh century BC both states, most of the time, coexisted peacefully.

The legacy of Sargon II was an empire at the height of its

A warm handshake between Shalmaneser III (right) and his contemporary, Marduk-Zakir-Shumi, the king of Babylon, decorates the throne pedestal from the throne room at Fort Shalmaneser. The Assyrian king had interceded on Marduk-Zakir-Shumi's behalf in the struggle for the crown that was waged between the Babylonian ruler and his upstart brother.

powers. The king built Dur Sharrukin, a new capital, at Khorsabad, the site where Botta began the rediscovery of ancient Assyria. Wars of conquest became fewer; the primary task of the Assyrians now was to defend what had already been gained, to keep the flow of tribute coming, and to ensure that no upstart neighbor or rebellious province disturb the imperial status quo. In 705 BC, in the course of putting down an uprising at Tabal, in the Taurus Mountains, Sargon was killed. Dur Sharrukin, not yet fully occupied, was now abandoned, probably considered unlucky because of its founder's death in battle. Trouble had been brewing in the Mediterranean coastal regions, as well as in Babylonia, to the east, and news of Sargon's

demise ignited revolts in both these quarters, which were put down with considerable, if expedient, savagery by his heir, Sennacherib.

In Babylon, the new king gave no quarter. Even to the Assyrians, the old city had been a holy place, home of gods who merited respect, and there is no record of any previous Assyrian sack of it. But Sennacherib had no scruples when it came to punishing this rebel place. He not only attacked it, in his own words, "as a whirlwind proceeds" but bragged of the thoroughness of his butchery, "Its inhabitants, young and old, I did not spare, and with their

Mighty doors open into the Treasury at Nimrud, in a watercolor (above) *by German archaeologist Walter Andrae for the stage set of the historical pantomime* Sardanapal, *based on the life of King Ashurbanipal. Lavishly costumed Assyrian courtiers pose on the set in publicity photos* (right) *for this 1908 Berlin production.*

106

corpses I filled the streets of the city." He set fire to the city and destroyed "its houses from their foundations to their roofs." Even the ashes and dust of the ruins, he went on to say, were taken away and distributed as souvenirs to loyalists elsewhere, or stored up in the temple of his own chief god, Assur, "in a covered jar."

Once the Babylonian uprising had been quelled and Sennacherib turned his attentions to the west, Syria and the Jewish kingdoms of Israel and Judah fared just as badly. City after city fell to Assyria's wrath. According to the Bible, Sennacherib sent a great army against the Judean king Hezekiah, who had rebelled against Assyrian hegemony. A brutal battle for the well-fortified frontier town of Lachish, located 25 miles southwest of Jerusalem, is pictorially chronicled by the victorious Assyrians on a series of reliefs sent by Austen Henry Layard to the British Museum *(pages 71-77),* and the event is mentioned in the Bible. Archaeologists have found strata showing heavy destruction at Lachish, as well as at Beersheba and Arad, cities about 50 miles south of Jerusalem. Sennacherib seemed unstoppable.

Jerusalem itself was under siege. A stone found at Nineveh records the story from the Assyrian point of view, hurling scorn at the king of Judah: "And Hezekiah of Judah who had not submitted to my yoke . . . him I shut up in Jerusalem his royal city like a caged bird. Earthworks I threw up against him, and anyone coming out of his city gate I made to pay for his crime. His cities which I had plundered I cut off from his land." The account that begins so fiercely, however, says nothing of battle, continuing instead with the observation that "the splendor of my majesty overwhelmed him," which it may well have done.

The inscription then lists the tribute paid by Hezekiah of 30 gold talents, "valuable treasures," and a number of his "male and female singers," as well as concubines and daughters. With surprising congruity on the amount of gold tribute, the Bible concurs that "the king of Assyria appointed unto Hezekiah king of Judah three hundred talents of silver and 30 talents of gold."

The Assyrian policy of relocating conquered peoples is also noted in the Bible: In the northern kingdom of Israel—home of 10 of the 12 tribes that constituted the ancient Jewish populace, and harder hit by the Assyrians than the southern kingdom of Judah—much of the population was taken to places unknown, never to return. These Israelites have become enshrined in legend, and in the memory of the Jewish people, as the ten lost tribes of Israel.

Back home in Assyria, Sennacherib moved his capital to Nineveh and turned his energies to the construction of a new building complex there,

which he dubbed "the palace without rival." It was intended as a monument to his glorious achievements. The edifice covered some two and one half acres of ground and was a symphony of dazzling white limestone, rare and fragrant woods, carved ivory, and trimmings of precious metals. Constructing it were deported or conscripted artisans and laborers from all the empire's corners, including Babylonia, Israel, and Judea, the mountains of Asia Minor, and the northwestern extremities of Iran. Every detail of its design and furnishing, from the reliefs upon its interior walls to its gardens of exotic flora and fauna, was meant as a statement of Sennacherib's greatness, the breadth of his conquests, and the solidity of his power.

Yet this temple to kingly grandeur was not without domestic comforts. Wells furnished with pulleys, buckets, and bronze chains supplied water. Conveniently adjacent to the throne room was a bathroom, its brick floor waterproofed with bitumen; into a depressed part of this floor were set several drainage holes with stone plugs. Ventilation came from a device called, by contemporary sources, a "breeze door," which may have been a grille or other form of adjustable air vent. Archaeologists excavating the palace have also

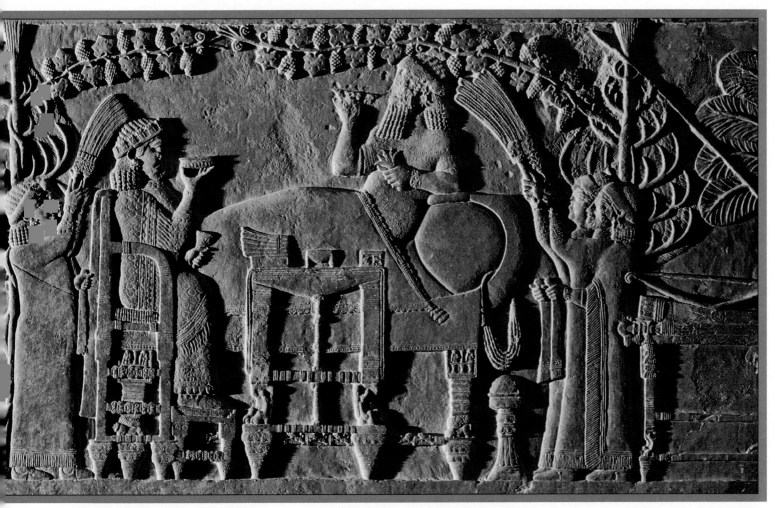

Surrounded by birds, grapevines, and palm and pine trees, reclining King Ashurbanipal takes refreshment in the garden with his queen, his bow and arrow set aside, in this relief from the seventh-century-BC palace at Nineveh. To the left, beyond the frond-waving servants, the severed head of his enemy, the vanquished Elamite king, hangs from a tree.

speculated about the long stone grooves, resembling a rudimentary form of railway track, that are set into the floor; the position and size of these channels suggest they may have been used to carry a large wheeled brazier across the room, to deliver heat to the occupants during Nineveh's sharp winters.

But Sennacherib did not have long to enjoy his splendid new quarters. In January 681 BC he met a sudden and violent death. According to some sources, he was murdered while at prayer in a Nineveh temple by the mutinous hand of one of his sons; other chronicles suggest that a giant stone image of a winged bull collapsed and crushed him during his devotions. Such a death, it was whispered, must have been divine retribution for some great sin, such as Sennacherib's destruction eight years earlier of Babylon, beloved of the gods. His successor, Esarhaddon, may well have agreed with this theory, for he was quick to make amends by reconstructing that sacred city. He also did his share of extending the empire, by moving into Egypt where he took Memphis, the Nubian-born pharaoh Taharqa's capital city, a repository of great wealth. Ironically, it was the treasure of Egypt that financed the rebuilding of Babylon.

Esarhaddon's heir, Ashurbanipal *(pages 108-109)*, fought hard to maintain control of his dominions and found himself at war on several fronts, including a rebellious Egypt. Between these battles he managed to create the spectacular library excavated at Nineveh, complete with bibliographical systems and an aggressive acquisitions policy: A surviving letter to a minion in Babylonia by the name of Kudurranu, for example, commands him to "seek out and send to me any rare tablets which are known to you and are lacking in Assyria." In various inscriptions Ashurbanipal boasted of his prowess as a scholar, claiming to have mastered a range of scribal arts, including the ability to read complex texts in several languages and to solve challenging mathematical problems.

In the summer of 612 BC, some 15 years after Ashurbanipal's death, a rebuilt and resuscitated Babylon would take revenge on its Assyrian desecrators. A combined assault by the Babylonians and their allies, the Medes, who occupied territory east of Assyria in the fertile valleys of western Iran, climaxed in a three-month siege of Nineveh. The Babylonians recorded their victory in the battle for the Assyrian capital in a cuneiform chronicle that was read by scholars in 1923.

Excavations in 1989-1990 by the University of California at Berkeley, led by British archaeologist David Stronach, at the Halzi Gate, an eight-towered stone entry to the southeastern corner of the city, have brought to light concrete evidence of Nineveh's final hours. Archaeolo-

Arms upraised to support a basket filled with earth, Ashurbanipal himself participates in rebuilding the Temple of Marduk at Babylon, as shown on a stele dating from 660 BC. This scene and similar depictions of such ancient ceremonies predating Sumer symbolize the king's religious duty to build and maintain the temples.

gists found signs of last-ditch defensive efforts, such as a stone dragged into position to block the enemy's passage, some rough attempts at patching crumbling walls, and the narrowing of the aperture within the city's gate. But the failure of these exertions was confirmed not only by ancient historians but also by Stronach, who discovered, at this imposing gate, a pile of the defenders' corpses, the remains of at least 12 people, frozen in their death-agonies. A boy, no older than 13, lay with an arrowhead still piercing his lower leg; another victim collapsed face downward; a third died with his arms outstretched and his face turned toward the sky.

With the fall of Nineveh, the monarchy fled to Harran, a city on a tributary of the Euphrates in what is now southern Turkey. There a new king, Ashuruballit, presided over the final days of the Assyrian empire. In 605 BC the Babylonians and their allies engaged the Assyrians at Carchemish, 50 miles west of Harran. Once again the Bible appears to fill in some of the gaps in the story: The pharaoh Necho was on his way to aid Assyria, Egypt's erstwhile bitter foe, now an ally, when he was intercepted by an army led by the Judean king Josiah, who wanted to prevent Necho's forces from reaching the battleground. In a fierce skirmish, Josiah was killed and Necho went on to establish an Egyptian base at Carchemish. There Egypt supported the weak, terminally wounded Assyrians until in 605 BC the Babylonians ousted the Egyptians from the area.

Assyria's enemies, once victims of its might, did not mourn its demise. They would, no doubt, have shared the view of the Hebrew prophet Zephaniah, "See what has befallen the joyous city who queened it without a care, and said in her heart: 'There is none like me.' How she has become a desert, a resort for the wild beasts! Whosoever shall pass by her will hiss and wave his hand."

But it would be left to less-judgmental observers—men such as Botta, Layard, Mallowan, and Muzahim—to uncover the evidence that might present a fuller picture of Assyria's story.

ODYSSEY OF THE MONOLITHS

Had French consul and archaeologist Paul Emile Botta been able to read cuneiform, he might have considered himself forewarned. "According to my heart's inclination," read dedicatory tablets left by Sargon II in the foundation walls of his palace at Khorsabad, "I have built palaces of ivory, maple, boxwood, mulberry, cedar, and pistachio trees. I have dressed their portals with animals sculpted in white stone. Whoever would destroy the creation of my hands, let Assur, the great lord, destroy his name and his posterity on earth."

Innocent of Sargon's malediction, Botta went on to lay claim to two of the monarch's many gypsum beasts—the human-headed, winged bulls that guarded both his palace and the city's gates. Unfortunately, Botta's effort to transport two of the colossi to Paris in 1846—a feat involving 600 men, was plagued by ill fortune. In fact, bad luck

has attended the movement of stone giants like these—some with lion traits—since ancient times, when the statues were installed throughout Khorsabad, Nineveh, and Nimrud.

Intended as protective guardians and spirits, the huge beasts no doubt awed their ancient beholders. To Austen Henry Layard in the 19th century, they were "mysterious emblems" symbolizing the intellect of man, the ubiquity of birds, and the strength of lions and bulls. Today, those colossi continue to cast their spell over whole new generations of viewers in some of the world's great museums.

Freed partially from the earth by French archaeologist Victor Place, two human-headed bulls still grace one of the gateways to Khorsabad in the 1853 photograph at right. Only one of the two bulls was destined to reach the Louvre; the other fell from its raft into the Tigris, never to be retrieved. Additional monoliths (above) came to light during 1933 excavations there.

MOVING STONES WITH MUSCLE POWER

Had it not been for the self-promotion of King Sennacherib, who left an exhaustive record of his exploits and deeds chiseled in stone at his palace in Nineveh, scholars today would be hard-pressed to determine just how the ancient Assyrians quarried, worked, and transported the multiton blocks of limestone that they used in creating their winged guardians.

Happily, however, Sennacherib chronicled steps in the making of a bull colossus in a se- ries of reliefs that were discovered in 1849 by Henry Layard in the king's palace. These reliefs show everything—from the laborers proceeding to the quarry to the cutting of the great stone block and the hauling of the partially sculpted statue to the palace. Once the stone arrived at its destination, the final carving was done. The drawings reproduced here were made from the reliefs themselves.

Supplementing the king's remarkable pictorial lessons are his cuneiform accounts—some inscribed on the bull-colossi bellies and between their hind legs—that describe in detail the types and sources of stone used. From such written evidence, researchers have learned that Sennacherib tapped a quarry in nearby Balatai, eschewing an older one at Tastiate across the Tigris, and thus forgoing a risky river journey for the stones. His father, Sargon II, is known to have lost at least one colossus to the river's unpredictable floodwaters.

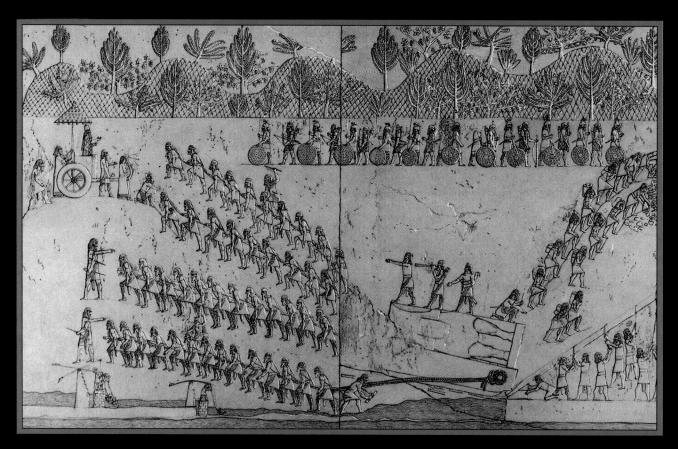

Straining to pull the monolith out of the quarry pit, four teams of laborers haul on massive ropes attached to the wooden sledge used to carry a winged bull. At upper left, King Sennacherib himself is seen superintending the operation from the comfort of his chariot, shaded by a parasol.

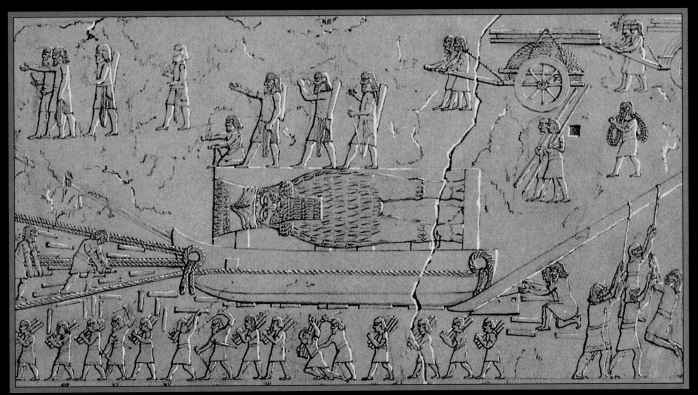

The heavily laden sledge moves wearily across dry land, nudged along by a crew of laborers plying a long wooden lever. Workers in the front place rollers under the vehicle in order to ease its passage, while King Sennacherib's supervisors, walking upon the colossus, direct the proceedings.

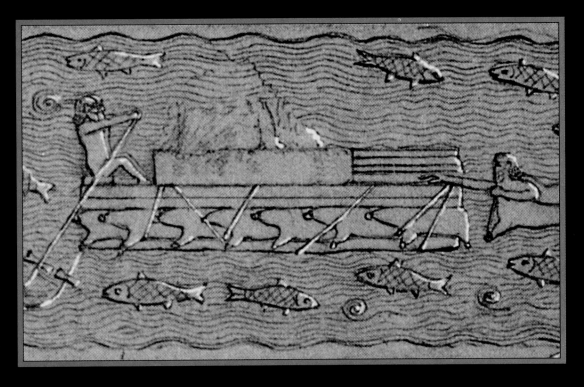

A raft buoyed by inflated animal skins conveys a block of stone from quarry to palace. Generally too bulky for river transport, the heavier colossi had to be dragged overland. Yet in the 19th century, Henry Layard resorted to the flotation method.

SHARING OUT THE TREASURES

In 1847, having unearthed more than a half-dozen pairs of winged colossi at Ashurnasirpal II's North West Palace in Nimrud, Henry Layard paused to reflect on the long sleep of the stone animals in the earth. "For 25 centuries," Layard wrote, "they had been hidden from the eye of man, and they now stood forth once more in their ancient majesty." Determined to share their splendor with his compatriots, Layard selected a lion and a bull from the palace's great central hall and arranged to have the monoliths shipped to the British Museum in London.

The journey—an 18-month odyssey from Nimrud to London via the Tigris, the Persian Gulf, and the Indian and Atlantic Oceans—was beset by several near-disasters: Layard's precious packing materials were stolen by Bedouins; the cart carrying the winged bull—which twice became mired in the soft earth en route to the river—was set upon by marauding Arabs; and both lion and bull were nearly pitched overboard in a tempest off Sri Lanka. But eventually the sculptures made it to England, there to attract crowds of the curious.

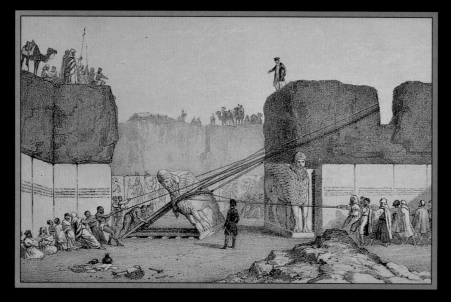

Layard directs the lowering of the 10-ton bull onto rollers from his post atop a ruined wall of Ashurnasirpal II's great central hall (left). In the pit, two teams of local workers struggle to balance a complex system of ropes and wooden braces supporting the descending monolith. Four or five feet from the ground, the ropes—by then smoking from the strain—gave way. Remarkably, the bull landed unscathed on its side, positioned for transport.

Swaddled in protective felt and mats, the bull inches riverward on a wheeled cart powered by some 300 toiling men. Leading the procession is Layard, riding horseback, followed by a band of native musicians. Onlookers line the route, while mounds containing the ruins of Nimrud loom in the distance. Initially, Layard yoked a team of buffalo to the cart, but the beasts—doubtless sensing the great weight behind them—stubbornly refused to move.

Armed guards stand protectively about the reclining bull, at last making its way down the Tigris to Basra. To construct the gargantuan raft, which required 600 goatskins and sheepskins to keep it afloat, Layard recruited a debt-ridden raftsman willing to chance what others said could not be done.

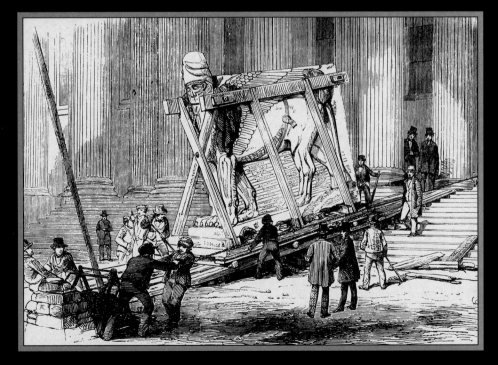

This engraving, published in The Illustrated London News, shows the mechanized conveyance of a human-headed, winged lion into the British Museum. One of a pair discovered flanking the doorway to Ashurnasirpal II's throne room, the lion arrived in 1852, more than three years after Layard's first bull and lion colossi made their London debut.

RESURRECTING SARGON'S BULL

The soil of Khorsabad had lain undisturbed for 74 years when, in 1928, archaeologist Edward Chiera of the Oriental Institute resumed the excavations begun by Botta and continued by Place.

While digging at the entrance to Sargon II's throne room, Chiera came upon a giant bull split into three large fragments. The figure—estimated to weigh 40 tons—was once coupled with the sculpture of a lion tamer that had been removed by Botta for display in the Louvre.

Magnificent even in three pieces, the sculpture was shipped to the United States. Too large to pass through railroad tunnels, it had to be rerouted along the tracks, journeying from New York to Chicago via New Or- leans. Reassembled, the statue was put on exhibit at Chicago's Oriental Institute.

In 1993 the Louvre had a replica made of the colossus for the museum's new Khorsabad Courtyard. There, after 150 years, the look-alike was joined together with the lion tamer to re-create the appearance of the original assemblage.

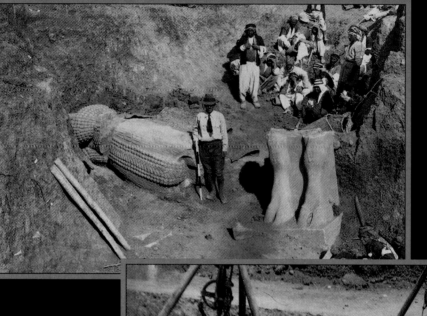

Standing at the entry to Sargon II's throne room, Chiera (left) poses be- tween the front legs and the torso of the broken gypsum bull. The trunk alone weighed some 20 tons. Below, workers aided by mechanical hoists position the wood-encased trunk on a trailer con- structed of cannon wheels and railroad ties left over from the First World War. The three-ton truck broke down four times on the way to the Tigris River.

A French worker in Chicago (top) *prepares a plaster casing designed to support and protect an underlying skin of silicone that forms the actual mold from which the copy of the Chicago bull will be made. Later, the silicone mold is peeled away from the face* (left). *Casing and mold were then taken to the Louvre where the replica was cast.*

ECHOES OF IMPERIAL GREATNESS

In 1991 the Louvre undertook ambitious plans to transfer its collection of Assyrian artifacts to the museum's new Richelieu Wing. The relocation, which was inspired in part by a desire to highlight the Louvre's Mesopotamian treasures, allowed the curators of the museum to redesign the exhibits in order to reflect the original settings in which the artworks were discovered. Thus was born the Louvre's Khorsabad Courtyard, an evocation of King Sargon II's own ceremonial courtyard, with stucco walls, burned-brick floors, and natural light.

Ranged with other works around the room's perimeter are Paul Emile Botta's two bull colossi (*right*) guarding a mock doorway—the one surviving bull from Place's ill-fated Khorsabad expedition, and a plaster copy made in 1857 to simulate its lost twin—and the cast of the Chicago bull, along with its lion-tamer mate and winged genie figures.

Traffic comes to a halt on the Rue de Rivoli outside the Louvre's Richelieu Wing as one of Botta's 30-ton bulls—encased in a steel frame—rides toward its new home in the museum's Khorsabad Courtyard.

Looking no worse for wear, Sargon's nearly 14-foot-tall winged bulls resume their eternal watch, in the Louvre's Khorsabad Courtyard. To facilitate their shipment from the Middle East to Paris, they were sawed in pieces by their discoverer, Botta.

A CITY BLESSED
BY
THE GODS

When Claudius James Rich went to see the ruins of Babylon in 1811, he traveled in grand style. He believed that to win the respect of the local populace, he had to put on a flamboyant show as he trekked along the arduous 50-mile route south from Baghdad. For two days, across dried-up canals and towering mounds, his caravan made its way, Rich in the lead on his horse, followed by a troop of hussars, or light cavalry, and 13 sepoy warriors from India, all of them decked out in their colorful regimental garb. Mounted on a horse-drawn carriage was a light cannon, known as a galloper gun, and bringing up the rear were 70 baggage-laden mules.

Rich's wife, Mary, accompanied him, but not nearly so pompously nor comfortably; she rode in a closed litter that rocked, like baggage, from a pole between two mules. The two maids she brought with her were penned into cagelike boxes and slung across the back of a single mule, the thinner woman perched on a pile of stones to balance the weight of her plumper traveling companion.

Although Rich was only 26 years old, the Babylon trip capped a lifetime of Middle Eastern studies. A child prodigy, Rich had been fascinated at the tender age of nine by some Arabic and Persian manuscripts and had proceeded to learn Arabic, Persian, Latin, Greek, Hebrew, Syrian, Turkish, Chaldean, and a little Chinese. Such linguistic skills earned him a position, at the age of 17, in the powerful

A symbol of Babylon's god Marduk, this bronze head of a horned snake-dragon was crafted in the sixth century BC and graced the tip of the pole of a chariot or scepter. The grooves along the figure's neck suggest that the piece was once covered with gold leaf.

East India Company, which managed Britain's trade interests throughout much of Asia, and in 1808 the newly married Rich had been appointed the company's representative in Baghdad. Previous postings had allowed him to indulge his curiosity about other civilizations: In Egypt, for example, not only had he perfected his Arabic and learned horsemanship and the use of a lance and scimitar from the warrior-like people known as Mamelukes, but he had also journeyed into Syria and Persia disguised as a tribesman.

Now he was compiling manuscripts and artifacts for a history of the Mesopotamian region, and it was inevitable that he would visit the remains of the legendary city whose very name had echoed through the centuries. The fifth-century-BC Greek historian Herodotus, who claimed to have visited Babylon, reported that "it surpasses in splendor any city of the known world." In the accounts of other classical writers, it was described as a marvel of size, pomp, and wealth. Within its walls stood the mighty ziggurat of Etemenaki—believed by some to be the original Tower of Babel *(pages 39-45)*—and many fabulous temples, as well as the Hanging Gardens, hailed by ancient writers as one of the Seven Wonders of the World. In the Bible, the city's very name became a byword for corruption and sinful excess, although the Judeans too fell under its influence.

As scholars have discovered from cuneiform inscriptions on countless clay tablets detailing the minutiae of daily life, Babylon was a thriving commercial center during its revival as a major power in the mid first millennium BC. Its empire stretched from the Persian Gulf to the borders of Egypt and along the Mediterranean coast of what today is Lebanon. In the bustling capital a cosmopolitan population of migrants from regions throughout the Middle East mingled, creating a dynamic mix of various cultural traditions in which developed the learning that would lay the foundations of modern astronomy, medicine, mathematics, and writing.

For all its glory, the city's brief flowering in what is known as the Neo-Babylonian era was less than 70 years, from 605 to 539 BC. Babylon was ruled for more than half of that time by the mighty Nebuchadnezzar II, whose ambitious building schemes created a capital of awe-inspiring grandeur.

The remote location of the ancient site was well known—if rarely seen—in the 19th century, and since the 12th century, Western travelers had left sketchy records of brief visits. The local Bedouin no-

Possibly used as a household icon, this two-inch, terra-cotta statuette of a mother holding an infant to her breast was modeled between 600 and 500 BC and unearthed in Babylon by German archaeologists in 1909. Such figures were believed to offer protection to the home and family.

mads still referred to Babylon's mounds by their ancient names— Babil and Kasr, or palace. Rich therefore had no doubt about what city he was exploring during the 10 days he measured, paced out, and sketched the immense swells, overgrown with tussocks of rank grass and set off by pools of brackish water. He rode from one end to the other of the vast site that stretched some five miles along the left bank of the Euphrates, naming each hillock and employing his accompanying troops to aid in the survey, while workers from a nearby village, digging out surviving bricks for their own use, sold him inscribed specimens for his collection.

The trip was exhilarating, yet there was little in the broken jumble to suggest the city's storied buildings. Most of the sunbaked mud bricks had crumbled back into earth; local people had, for centuries, quarried the site for any reusable building materials, and great piles of rubble had accumulated over the remnants. As the German archaeologist Robert Koldewey, Babylon's first long-term excavator, would observe a century later, "To those accustomed to Greece and its remains, it is a constant surprise to have these mounds pointed out as ruins. Here are no blocks of stone, no columns; even in excavation there is only brickwork."

After his visit, Rich published two accounts of his detailed observations of the site, the second after his return to Babylon in 1817 to check measurements that he had made on the earlier trip. Both books stirred the public imagination and also earned him the respect of scholars. Nonetheless he could not exclude a note of dismay, admitting, "I announce no discovery, I advance no interesting hypothesis." Instead he simply described what he saw. Any attempt to decipher the remote site, he wrote, would lead only to "inextricable confusion."

Yet it was Rich's legacy that would lead scholars out of the "confusion": The young explorer died bravely, even nobly, in 1821, after contracting cholera while nursing victims of an epidemic in the Iranian city of Shiraz. He left the world not only his shining personal example, but also his collection of ancient manuscripts and artifacts, including some of the first specimens of cuneiform inscriptions seen in Europe, which went to the British Museum. There they stimulated the methodical study of ancient Mesopotamia by 19th-century British, French, and German academics and archaeologists.

The eventual excavator of Babylon would be one of a new breed of trained, scientific scholars far removed from earlier amateurs such as Rich. Robert Koldewey, who dug there between 1899 and 1917, was a man whose good-humored, high-spirited disposition belied his patient, methodical approach to his work. A trained excavator, with the experience of digs in Greece, Italy, and Syria, he would take archaeology to new levels of precision.

A white-suited Robert Koldewey strikes a jaunty pose at his expedition's headquarters in Babylon. Behind the good-humored German archaeologist are shelves crammed with artifacts recovered during his digs, which he conducted each year between 1899 and 1917.

The inspiration for Koldewey's dig may have occurred during his travels in 1887, when he spent two days wandering through Babylon's ruins and was intrigued to find a few fragments of brightly colored, glazed bricks. A closer examination, however, would have to wait another decade until Koldewey returned, looking for a potential site for long-term excavation. More blue, red, yellow, and white brick pieces convinced him and his superiors at the Royal Museums in Berlin that this was their spot. On March 26, 1899, Koldewey's team cut the first exploratory trench across the eastern side of the Kasr, a mile-long mound near the Euphrates River, where ancient reports located Babylon's royal palace.

Early digging revealed the source of the brick chips when the team found the ends of two parallel walls marking the sides of a street, more than 60 feet wide and almost 600 feet long, which ran south into the mass of ruins. This roadway was edged in a red stone called breccia and paved with white flagstones, each about three feet square, still polished and slippery from the sandals that had once walked along them. The whole elaborate path sat on a base of brick and asphalt atop a foundation of mud, sand, and rubble. This structure raised the sloping street 39 to 46 feet above the surrounding plain.

But it was the walls that once rose about 35 feet alongside this astonishing road that delighted the excavators. They had been a striking shade of blue, lined with friezes made of fire-baked bricks enameled in bright colors. Along the azure walls, rows of lions, each about six-and-a-half feet long, in white, yellow, and red—perhaps as many as 60 on each side of the street—had marched toward the city. This imposing road entered the city walls at the magnificent Ishtar Gate (pages 151-157).

For would-be attackers, Koldewey noted, the enclosed street was "a real pathway of death," where they would have been easy prey for the city's defenders perched on the walls to either side. But defense was not the primary purpose of this ornate approach to Babylon's center. The ancient cuneiform tablets, from

In this sketch from the Babylon expedition's guest book, Koldewey's colleague Walter Andrae pokes sly fun at a German museum director's fanciful characterization of Babylon as a bleeding king's daughter in need of assistance. The drawing shows Koldewey (left) and Andrae helping the stricken figure quench its thirst in the waters of the Euphrates. Two visitors to the dig on February 23, 1901, have wryly noted that "Babylon has a great future in its past."

Seen from the northwest in this sweeping aerial view, the ruins of Nebuchadnezzar's trapezoidal main palace at Babylon still hint of ancient magnificence. The rectangular structure at far left was the temple of Ninmah; running diagonally to its right were the Processional Way and the Ishtar Gate. Lined up just above the cruciform excavation of the gate are the foundations of what some believe were the fabled Hanging Gardens of Babylon. The cleared rectangular area at upper left was the ruler's throne room.

which Koldewey had already gleaned a sketchy knowledge of the city, had described the pomp and pageantry that had filled the magnificent passageway during Babylon's New Year's festival each spring. Then it would become a sacred path for the ceremonial entry of the god Marduk, in a ritual celebrating the renewal of nature and believed essential to ensuring the continued prosperity of the capital. Koldewey dubbed the road the Processional Way.

The beginning of the Babylonian year fell in the month called Nisan, straddling today's March and April and containing the spring equinox, when day and night are of equal length. During the 11-day ceremonies of Akitu, the New Year's festival, the fate of Babylon and its inhabitants was decided by Marduk, who had been gradually elevated from a minor position among the gods to become the major deity not just of the city but of all of southern Mesopotamia. Assyriologists have deciphered from cuneiform tablets many of the details of Akitu, including the sacrifices performed and the recitation of an epic poem recounting Marduk's triumph in battle over the forces of Chaos in the creation of the world *(pages 60-61)*.

The New Year's festival was also a renewal of the kingship, a time when the monarch had to prove his worthiness to rule yet another year. On the fifth day of Akitu, the king went to the New Year's temple, which lay outside the city's walls. It was the one time the king was allowed inside this sanctuary, where he was ritually humbled before the statue of the god: He could enter only without his royal regalia, and in that holiest of places, he had to swear that he had not offended the gods in the past year and to call for Marduk's blessing on the city. A fertility rite took place within a temple, which scholars believe included a physical union between the king and a priestess, perhaps symbolizing the special relationship between earthly and heavenly rulers.

On the 11th and final day, the king and the statue of Marduk in their respective chariots led a great train of priests and other idols along the Processional Way. By the time the parade reached Babylon's gorgeously decorated gates, almost everyone had left the city to reenter triumphantly, the fertility of the next year assured, the power of Marduk reaffirmed, and the king secure on his throne.

The credit for building Babylon's splendid processional walk was established in a cuneiform inscription: "Aibur-shabu, the roadway of Babylon, I filled up with a high filling for the procession of the great

His left hand gripping a rod and ring, symbols of kingly power, the richly garbed god Marduk stands with a snake-dragon in this drawing taken from an incised image on a lapis lazuli cylinder seal found in the remains of a Babylonian house. As the patron god of Babylon, Marduk grew in popularity as the city increased its wealth and influence.

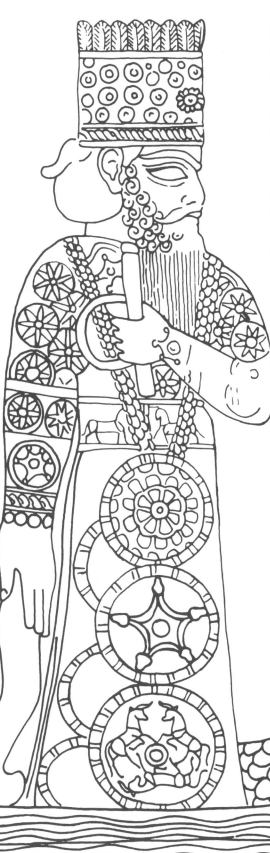

lord Marduk, and with slabs of breccia and mountain stone I have made Aibur-shabu suitable for the procession of his divine self." The author of this account left his name inscribed along the sides of the broad flagstones where, once the stones had been laid, none but the all-seeing eyes of Marduk himself might read the words: Nebuchadnezzar, king of Babylon.

When Koldewey first publicized his find, the world thrilled to the very mention of the name Nebuchadnezzar II, well known from classical accounts and from the Bible, where he achieved infamy as the king who sacked Jerusalem and led thousands of Jews into captivity. But this greatest monarch of the Neo-Babylonian period, who ruled from 605 to 562 BC, had also left inscriptions on countless bricks, testifying to his tireless construction in the city. His buildings rose above earlier settlements that, Koldewey discovered, now lay out of reach beneath the modern underground water level.

As the son of Nabopolassar, the king who was responsible for destroying Nineveh in 612 BC and fatally weakening Assyrian power, Nebuchadnezzar II took it upon himself to finally defeat the Assyrians at the battle of Carchemish, on the upper Euphrates, in 605 BC. He then hurried home, where his father was dying, in order to secure his inheritance.

Nebuchadnezzar was descended from the Chaldeans, another group that, like the Amorites and Kassites, had migrated to southern Mesopotamia, eventually founding a dynasty and breathing new life into the region. Upon his accession to the throne, Nebuchadnezzar turned his attention to strengthening the city's defenses. In 648 BC, only 43 years before his reign, Babylon had been captured by the Assyrians, led by Ashurbanipal, and military attack remained a constant danger. The new king therefore enlarged the thick defensive walls and wide canals that ringed the city to enclose an area of about three square miles, which, historians estimate, held a population of some 200,000.

The city was also threatened by flooding from the Euphrates River, and Nebuchadnezzar lined canals and walls with waterproof bitumen to provide added protection against breakthrough or seepage. The river was, for all its potential overflow, Babylon's lifeblood. Harnessed

In this Babylonian map of the earth, the Salt Sea circles the known world, with the west at top. Babylon appears as a rectangular box just above the center and below an arc of mountains that are the source of the Euphrates River, shown flowing from top to bottom. Beyond the encompassing sea lie fabulous regions—one of them the home of Ziusudra, survivor of the Great Flood of Babylonian myth—that are described in the cuneiform text above the map.

in canals, its waters compensated for the region's scant rainfall to irrigate the plains. Herodotus observed of the plains that "so great is the fertility of the grain fields that they normally produce crops of two-hundredfold," or 200 times the weight of the grain used as seed.

The river also lay at the heart of Babylon's commercial wealth. Busy trade routes crossed the empire, heading toward the Mediterranean, into Asia Minor, and down through Arabia, and tribute arrived from the rich provinces of the Middle East. Cargo-bearing ships sailed down the Euphrates to dock at Babylon's bustling quay, where Herodotus reported they would be unloaded and dismantled, to be carried back upriver on the backs of donkeys when the strength of the current effectively prevented ships from sailing upstream. An abundance of textual evidence, however, documents that these large wooden barges were towed against the flow, along the shorelines of rivers and canals, using ropes pulled by men or attached to oxen or mules.

From the provident Euphrates too came the city's building material. Stone and wood were rare in the plains, and the people of Babylon turned instead to the alluvial soil of the riverbanks to supply what was probably the ancient world's greatest brick-making industry. Gangs of workmen toiled in the heat, packing thousands of regular wooden molds with mud that the relentless sun dried into durable building blocks. On the backs of some of the blocks, Koldewey saw the handprints of the men who had patted them into shape some 2,400 years before.

For the excavators, these bricks dictated new archaeological techniques. The key to success lay in tracing the walls, which had crumbled onto the surrounding earth. To this end Koldewey assembled a team of some 250 men, who developed a highly systematic method of wall clearance, universally adopted by later archaeologists: First they would survey the ground, searching for intact mud bricks or any subtle change in the color of the soil that might indicate the course of a wall. When such evidence was found, some workers would carefully pick layers of soil off the wall, while others carried this dirt away in a basket to a miniature railway that dumped it into an unimportant corner of the site.

It was essential that every find be noted just as it was unearthed, for, once exposed, the intact mud bricks buried under the dissolved ones would rapidly deteriorate. The best opportunity that archaeologists would have to study the city, therefore, was at the moment of discovery.

Despite the oppressive summer heat—temperatures sometimes reached as high as 130 degrees Fahrenheit in the shade—Koldewey pressed on. But in his 12th season, in 1910, he faced a serious problem: Near the Processional Way, in what once had been the heart of the city, was the supposed location of Marduk's great temple, called Esagila, "the temple that raises its head," by the Babylonians in honor of its lofty structure. But the spot now lay buried beneath a massive mound called Amran ibn Ali, the name of a heroic figure in Islamic history.

An exploratory shaft, dug into the center of the hill, was sunk lower daily without any result. Finally, almost 70 feet down, the diggers hit something solid. By amazing luck, Koldewey had struck a paved floor bearing inscriptions of the ancient Assyrian kings Ashur-

Dating from the time of Nebuchadnezzar, the text of this seven-inch-long fired-clay cylinder tells of the construction of a temple and was intended to carry its message to the gods. In closing, the builder implores the god Ninkarrak to "look kindly upon the work of my hands. The joy of my heart is given as a gift. Before Shamash and Marduk may my works be judged. Speak on my behalf!"

banipal and Esarhaddon, which positively identified the site as Esagila. Nevertheless, the team had to clear away more than a million cubic feet of rubble to expose even a part of the structure. Eventually, they resorted to tunneling around the walls to learn the temple's vast dimensions of 185,000 square feet.

Inside, according to his own records, Nebuchadnezzar had created a dazzling chamber fit for the deity, "I made its walls gleam like the sun, with shining gold. With lapis lazuli and alabaster I clothed the inside of the temple." Now, however, beyond its enormous size, there was little left to suggest the building's grandeur, for Esagila had been thoroughly plundered centuries before.

Koldewey knew that the great builder, Nebuchadnezzar, had lived and worked in luxurious surroundings in the largest of Babylon's three principal palaces, the Southern Palace, which he called "the seat of my kingdom, the bond of the vast assemblage of all mankind, the dwelling-place of joy and gladness." The king boasted of laying its foundations "on Earth's wide breast with bitumen and bricks; mighty trunks of cedars I brought from Lebanon, the bright forest for its roofing; I caused it to be surrounded with a mighty wall of bitumen and brick, the royal command, the lordly injunction I caused to go forth from it."

As Koldewey excavated the building, located just inside the monumental Ishtar Gate, he learned from inscriptions that the site comprised two structures, an immense older one, reconstructed by Nebuchadnezzar, and an extension to the north that the king added later. The older building had been erected by Nabopolassar in traditional Mesopotamian fashion around a series of five courtyards, which, together with adjacent rooms, were used respectively for a military garrison, administrative offices, state affairs, the King's private chambers, and the women's quarters. These last were grouped around the innermost courtyard and housed not only Nebuchadnezzar's queen but also a harem of concubines sent from all parts of the Babylonian empire.

The throne room of Nebuchadnezzar, some 180 feet long and 197 feet wide, faced north onto the largest courtyard, in order to minimize the sun's heat. Koldewey discovered that the chamber's exterior facade, some 40 feet high and 184 feet wide, had at one time been decorated with elaborate glazed-brick friezes. Again, careful deduction allowed him to piece together the original scene with its colorful parading animals against a dark blue background, reminiscent of

Still standing near the spot where it was uncovered in Nebuchadnezzar's main palace, this 8½-foot-long basalt statue of a lion trampling a prostrate man is thought to have been carved by Hittites or Assyrians. It may have been brought to Babylon for display as a war prize.

those along the Processional Way. (With financial support from the Iraqi government, much of this vast, extraordinary palace has now been reconstructed.)

Although Koldewey had managed to plumb the long-lost secrets of the Processional Way, Esagila, and the great throne room of Nebuchadnezzar, one of Babylon's most enduring mysteries remained unsolved. And then, while exploring the northeastern corner of the palace, the archaeologist uncovered a series of curious cells with vaulted roofs; in their midst was an ancient well. No other arched constructions had yet been found in Mesopotamia. For Koldewey, there could be little doubt that he had hit upon the legendary Hanging Gardens of Babylon.

A handful of Greek travelers, writing between the fourth and first centuries BC, had left accounts of this garden, built on an artificial hillside of rising tiers by Nebuchadnezzar to please his Median wife, who, in the Babylonian plains, was homesick for her mountainous native landscape. Upon each tier the deep soil was said to have been thickly planted with trees. According to an observer writing around 400 BC, some of these trees were as tall as 50 feet, and "a distant spectator of these groves would suppose them to be woods nodding on their mountains."

Significantly—to Koldewey, at least—the walls of the 14 arched rooms were uncommonly thick, obviously intended to bear a great weight. Also, the ruins contained numerous fragments of hewn stone, a material rare in Babylon. Consulting ancient sources—both cuneiform tablets and the work of the five classical Greek writers who had described the Hanging Gardens—Koldewey found that hewn stone is reported to have been used in only two places, in the construction of the north wall of the Kasr, Nebuchadnezzar's main palace complex, and of the Hanging Gardens.

For all that, later archaeologists have challenged Koldewey's claim that he had found the famous but elusive gardens. An archive of cuneiform tablets that Koldewey discovered in the vaulted rooms proved to be lists of rations of oil and barley, suggesting that they might have been mere storerooms. Moreover, the site is far from the river or any water source other than a single well, and its location in the palace meant that anyone visiting it would have had to pass through the private apartments of the king and his harem. As an alternate location of the gardens, some modern scholars have proposed a possible site alongside the Euphrates, where excavations have revealed deep drains possibly used for irrigating such a structure.

Puzzling is the absence of any mention of the Hanging Gardens in Babylonian cuneiform records, normally so assiduous in recording Nebuchadnezzar's buildings. Neither does this attraction appear in the account of Herodotus. Despite a century of archaeological investigation, the mystery remains: Not only does no one know where the gardens were, but it is also not certain whether they ever existed at all.

The vaulted rooms, however, held another remarkable secret, one relating to Jewish history, although it would take a while to come to light. The cuneiform tablets Koldewey had uncovered at the site were recorded, numbered, and sent back to Berlin for eventual deciphering. There they lay in packing cases in the museum basement until 1933, when the Assyriologist Ernst Weidner began their translation. It seemed a thankless task, yielding nothing but mundane bookkeeping records. But Weidner plodded on, and his persistence paid off when he came across four receipts for the issue of supplies. These detailed the rations of one Ja-u-kinu. Some experts believe that

Fashioned of color-glazed brick, this 40-foot-tall, speculative reconstruction of the facade of Nebuchadnezzar's throne room stands in a gallery of Berlin's Vorderasiatisches Museum. The lions, perhaps symbolic of the goddess Ishtar and royalty, and portions of the border are original; their reassembly was aided by matching up coded marks made on the bricks by ancient Babylonian craftsmen.

this was Jehoiachin, king of Judah, who, according to the biblical account, had been led into captivity in Babylon by Nebuchadnezzar. In 1955 a further twist to the story came from an obscure 2,500-year-old cuneiform tablet in the British Museum, where the scholar Donald Wiseman deciphered a few phrases in the records of the Babylonian royal house concerning the capture of a Judean king, "He [Nebuchadnezzar] encamped over against the city of the Judeans and conquered it. He took the king prisoner." Although the tablet did not name the captive ruler, some observers have speculated that it was another reference to Jehoiachin.

In the biblical account, Nebuchadnezzar had invaded Jerusalem twice during his constant military campaigns to protect the valuable provinces of the empire. His first assault came in 597, when he besieged Jerusalem, deported King Jehoiachin and many of the Jews to Babylon, and installed Zedekiah, Jehoiachin's uncle, to rule the state as a vassal of Babylonia. The Second Book of Kings bemoans the consequences of the Babylonian victory: "And he carried away all Jerusalem and all the princes, and all the mighty men of valor, even ten thousand captives, and all the craftsmen and smiths: none remained, save the poorest sort of the people of the land."

Despite this devastating blow and warnings against insurrection by the prophet Jeremiah, the remaining impoverished Judeans increasingly denounced Babylon and demanded repayment of all tribute the king had exacted. Finally, the Bible relates, the Judean king Zedekiah "rebelled against the king of Babylon." In 588 BC the Babylonians marched into Judea with a strong army and, after an 18-month siege, took Jerusalem. The fallen city was plundered and put to the torch, and more of its population was led into exile in Babylonia. Jerusalem's great temple, built by King Solomon, was destroyed, and Judah became a Babylonian province, bringing to an end the 400-year rule of the house of David.

To the captive Jewish residents of Babylon who worshiped a single, all-powerful, invisible god, the natives' adoration of idols must have seemed, as the Bible calls it, an "abomination." But as the New Year's festival has demonstrated, the Babylonians regarded the statues of their gods as much more than mere figures of stone. They devoutly believed that the gods were actually present in some form in the idols created to represent and honor them. Meals of choice food were ceremonially laid before the statues, and curtains were drawn while the deities ate; temple servants soothed the gods with singing and music from flutes, panpipes, and lutes. Within the temple of Marduk, the powerful god—attended by his consort, the goddess Sarpanitum, and various servants—was dressed in rich raiments and precious stones. Herodotus recorded that Marduk's statue, 15 feet high, was made of 22 tons of gold and that the devoted Babylonians offered something like two and a half tons of valuable frankincense every year on the nearby altar.

The Mesopotamian environment fairly swarmed with deities—some of them seen as family groups of husband, wife, and children—whom it was humanity's duty to serve. There were gods of the moon and sun, of fertility and war; patron gods of various cities and professions; as well as personal gods who protected individuals. The Euphrates itself was regarded as a deity, and it was a crime to spit or urinate in the river.

Moreover, malevolent spirits seemingly lurked everywhere. Buried beside the thresholds of homes were consecrated clay figures, often of guard dogs with names such as "Loud of bark" and "Don't stop to think, bite!" They had been placed there to ward off evil demons and the ghosts of those who had died violent deaths. Sacred amulets worn as jewelry served the same purpose. Such spirits, the Babylonians believed, lay in wait to torment those who failed in their devotions to the gods. Only continual worship, ritual, and sacrifice would guard the individual from demons and the city from collapse.

The beneficiaries of such fears were Babylon's reported 1,179 temples, which were centers of great wealth. The temples owned almost half of all Babylonian land, and their staffs included numerous scribes, whose writing kept alive ancient Sumerian rituals and traditions, and a host of administrators who looked after the

This beautifully turned and polished 15-inch scepter was found by Koldewey in a Babylonian house in 1900 and had probably originally come from a shrine to the god Marduk. The scepter's bronze core had corroded, causing the surrounding pieces of black agate—commonly called onyx—to separate. Curators were able to make a complete reconstruction of the piece, although it is not certain whether each section was placed in the same position as in the original.

temples' complex business affairs and managed their farms. Operating almost as a state within a state, the rich temples largely governed their own affairs, a situation tolerated by Chaldean monarchs in exchange for the 20 percent tax they collected on all sacred revenues.

Temple lands were tended by tenants or serfs who maintained essential irrigation canals, grazed cattle, and gathered the harvest. Such workers were not always assiduous in their duties, and one letter admonished an administrator, "Do not be negligent with regard to your work and the work of the farmers. Don't you know that these are people whom one has to drive?" The author of another complaint to a temple official vented his frustration at the lack of an adequate labor force: "There are no hired men here; they all left before the month of Duzu. Also, the temple servants who you keep sending to me have no provisions with them. They work for five days and then run away, while men hired by the month earn five shekels of silver per man each month." Revealing the annoyance that lower bureaucrats probably have felt from time immemorial toward their superi-

One of the famous Seven Wonders of the World, the Hanging Gardens of Babylon are shown in their heyday, as sketched by Koldewey, who identified the site of the ruins in 1913. Other scholars, however, have proposed alternate locations or even questioned the very existence of the gardens, noting that they are not mentioned in contemporary Babylonian texts.

ors, he added, "You are impatient, but I am likewise impatient, especially since you keep on saying: 'I am coming myself and will do the work.' " Exasperated, he continued, "If you want to, send me word and I will leave. Then come here and do the work yourself."

Whatever the labor problems, the temples thrived, benefiting not just from rents on their land and taxes from the community but also from rich gifts. Small boxes stood at the entrances to the sanctuaries in which worshipers dropped pieces of silver, but donations came in other forms as well. On a single day, a tablet from one temple records, among other offerings, the receipt of 70 birds and ducks, 40 sheep, eight lambs, two bulls, one bullock, four wild boars, three ostrich eggs, dates, figs, raisins, and 54 containers of beer and wine. An anxious letter writer apologizes for his inability to make his donation, "My lord should not be annoyed because the sheep and goats are late in coming. The king has taken away my sons and I have been sick now for two years. I am in a dangerous condition and cannot possibly rise from my bed."

Current accumulation of wealth was only one part of the immense riches that might fill temple treasuries, for valuable items were preserved for thousands of years. This was demonstrated by a curious incident during British archaeologist Leonard Woolley's 1922-1934 excavation in Ur. Early in the dig, Woolley happened upon a small temple that dated from the city's last days but whose walls seemed much older. Suspecting that the building might lie over the top of an earlier structure, Woolley ordered his workmen to pull up a dozen bricks from the floor to test his theory. The local diggers, having been taught never to disturb any brick in place, concluded that this sacrilege could only mean that Woolley was searching for buried gold. To Woolley's amazement, within a few minutes one of them shouted, "We have found the gold." Coincidentally, beneath the slabs lay a hoard of gold jewelry, including earrings, beads, and pendants. No amount of persuading could convince the workmen that the discovery had been a happy accident. The dates of these pieces were astounding, spanning a period from Nebuchadnezzar's time back through the Old Babylonian era, even to the reign, in the third millennium BC, of Sargon of Akkad.

According to the myths Babylon had inherited from ancient Sumer, the gods so devoutly served and enriched had once dwelt on earth but had later ascended to the heavens. Since events in the sky were

The dog-faced demon god Pazuzu peers over the edge of this graphic, five-inch cast-bronze plaque designed to ward off the demon Lamashtu. The figures across the top of the plaque represent the main Babylonian gods; in the following row is a group of animal-headed protective beings. Next, a sick person is attended by fish-garbed priests. At bottom, Pazuzu drives Lamashtu back to the underworld. Lamashtu was especially harmful to pregnant women, unborn children, and newborn babies, who often wore protective amulets depicting Pazuzu around their necks.

thought to have a direct bearing on those on earth, diviners looked to the celestial bodies for clues to the heavenly will. Eclipses, the colors of stars, and the direction of the winds could all be seen as offering advice about state policy, private lives, and agriculture.

Sometime around the eighth century BC, significant changes occurred: Babylonians watching the skies for supernatural signs began making precise observations and writing them down, a practice that continued for more than 350 years. Harnessing their sophisticated mathematics to the accumulation of celestial records, eventually they were able to predict eclipses of the Sun and the Moon, and the movements of planets, with an accuracy that European astronomers would not match until the 18th century. These astronomical studies also led to a division of the day into hours, while arithmetical calculations, using a sexagesimal system of counting, which is based on the number 60, split the hours into minutes and seconds and the circle into 360 degrees.

In observatories throughout southern Mesopotamia, using only hollow tubes for sighting, astronomers divided the sky into three zones, recording and naming the visible stars in each. They were able to calculate, with astonishing precision, the relative distances of the stars from each other as the stars wheeled through the sky. It is from this process that the 12 signs of the zodiac evolved, and around the fifth century BC people began the casting of personal horoscopes in a manner similar to that still popular today.

Among the heavenly phenomena studied in Babylonian observatories was the cycle of the Moon, which formed the basis of a calendar of 12 months of 30 days each and dictated Babylon's religious and agricultural timetable. The calendar was far from perfect, since a total of 360 days meant that additional periods called intercalary months had to be inserted every few years in order to keep the calendar in harmony with the seasons.

To the Greeks, who by the sixth century BC had assimilated many of the achievements of Babylonian astronomy and later passed them on to the Roman world, the very word Chaldean came to signify "astronomer." Similarly, they absorbed the accomplishments of Babylonian mathematicians, whose work had originally been prompted by practical concerns, such as everyday needs for measuring, the determination of compound interest on loans, and the proportions of chemical compounds required for manufacturing. As Babylonian society grew more complex, the demand arose for more-intricate calculations. Even in the Old Babylonian era, school texts had contained tables for multiplying and dividing; for finding

This baked-clay face of the demon Humbaba is formed to look like a swirling pattern of animal entrails, which were frequently examined by Babylonian seers for omens of future events. Measuring about three inches tall, the figure is inscribed on the back with the incomplete warning, "If the entrails look like the face of Humbaba . . ."

squares and square roots, cubes and cube roots, and reciprocals; and for exponential functions, geometric ideas, and numerous other sophisticated mathematical notions. These concepts are believed to have provided a foundation for early Greek mathematicians, such as Pythagoras. Medical science too progressed from magical exorcism designed to drive away the demons who caused illness, helped by the application of noxious ointments, to an increasing reliance on techniques of healing and the application of therapeutic remedies, a forerunner of the practices established by the fifth-century Greek Hippocrates, hailed as the founder of medicine.

Even as these sciences were progressing, new circumstances were threatening a revered, ancient element of Mesopotamian learning—the cuneiform script. Everything of importance was typically written down—from royal chronicles to personal letters, from inscriptions to receipts and regulations—but the knowledge of cuneiform, comprising some 600 characters, was relatively complicated and scribes required extensive training.

By Nebuchadnezzar's time the scribal tradition had been under challenge for years. Among the hordes of cuneiform records discovered in Babylon, some business accounts had been amended with memos in a language entirely different from the traditional Akkadian—Aramaic. This change reflects the growing presence of the Arameans, originally a nomadic people from the Syrian desert who spoke a Semitic vernacular. Since the late second millennium BC, they had been influential traders throughout the region between the Mediterranean and the Persian Gulf, where many ultimately settled on the plains of southern Mesopotamia.

When keeping their own records, the Arameans did not write in cuneiform, but instead used a script, adopted about 1100 BC, based on a 22-character alphabet developed earlier, probably in Canaan. It would gradually spread to Mediterranean and Aegean countries, carried by the seafaring Phoenicians. Unlike cuneiform, which could only be inscribed on wet clay, the new script was suitable for writing on a range of surfaces, such as papyrus, wax, or clay. Educated Babylonians and temple scribes had long resisted switching to Aramaic writing, even though traders were picking it up and it was fast becoming an accepted script in commercial transactions. Anyone could learn the short Aramaic alphabet, and its spread was especially rapid among nonliterate people. Despite scribal resistance, its ease of use ultimately guaranteed the Aramaic script's universal acceptance in the region. In the Mesopotamian north, the Assyrians had recognized the utility of Aramaic writing during the eighth century BC and had decreed a special status for both spoken language and script. As the script's popularity spread among the traders, so Aramaic speech grew to be adopted as the lingua franca of international commerce and diplomacy throughout the region, replacing Akkadian. Centuries later, Aramaic would be the mother tongue of Jesus, as it was of most people in the Middle East.

More immediate and drastic changes occurred in 562 BC, when Nebuchadnezzar died suddenly: The throne passed, after seven years of short-lived monarchs, to Nabonidus, who was brought to power in 555 BC by a rebellion among palace officials. The diplomat son of a high-ranking priestess of the moon god, Sin, the new king proclaimed himself a commoner on inscribed clay cylinders, "I am Nabonidus who have not the honor of being a somebody; kingship is not within me." The Babylonians readily accepted Nabonidus's nonroyal lineage, for they believed, as was expressed in the New Year's ritual, that kingship was a gift of the gods and not necessarily an inherited right.

Nabonidus, like Nebuchadnezzar, was an enthusiastic builder. To gain support for his imperial ambitions, he harkened back to the early days of Babylonian greatness. His ceaseless search for antiquities would earn him, from today's scholars, the label of royal archae-

Wielding a lengthy scepter, Babylon's last native king, Nabonidus, appears in relief on this stele, whose inscription tells, among other things, of a return to bountiful harvests after a time of drought. In front of the king are symbols of the planet Venus, the sun, and the moon, representing the deities Ishtar, Shamash, and Sin—the last particularly revered by Nabonidus.

Nabonidus's son, Belshazzar, is startled to see a disembodied hand writing on the wall during a feast at his palace in this painting by the 17th-century artist Rembrandt. Though the actual message was in Aramaic, Rembrandt wrote it in Hebrew letters. The cryptic inscription indicated that Babylon would fall to the Persians.

ologist. He took pride in adhering closely to tradition. His inscriptions declared that he restored ancient buildings exactly as they were, "not a finger's breadth beyond or behind." At Ur, Leonard Woolley discovered that Nabonidus had not just rebuilt the city's ancient ziggurat but also, in some cases, reconstructed buildings only recently restored by Nebuchadnezzar. He concluded that the new king was expressing his disapproval of his predecessor's innovations by returning the structures to their original forms.

Records show that Nabonidus had constantly searched in the foundations of temples he was rebuilding for ancient sources that would testify to the sanctity of the land. Woolley found further evidence of this veneration of the past beneath the floor of the residence of Nabonidus's daughter, the high priestess of Sin in the temple at Ur. There Woolley had been puzzled by a small collection of artifacts 700 to 1,600 years older than the building itself. These included a Kassite boundary slab from about 1400 BC, a fragment of a statue, and a votive stone. Eventually Woolley concluded that the priestess had maintained her own museum, with the exhibits carefully cataloged on a clay cylinder.

The king's extolling of ancient ways also found an outlet in his religious activities, which some of his contemporaries condemned as heretical. Like his mother and daughter, he was a worshiper of Sin, the moon god, one of the major Mesopotamian gods in earlier times. In contrast, Marduk's elevation to the top of the Babylonian pantheon had occurred relatively late. By returning the moon god to what the king saw as his rightful place in the heavenly hierarchy, Nabonidus was probably also trying to create an imperial religion. Such a faith might well have served as a unifying force for the Babylonian empire, had the king been more capable in its defense.

As Nabonidus relates on a stele found in 1956 in Harran, an ancient commercial and religious center, Marduk appeared to him in a dream early in his reign and commanded him to rebuild the neglected temple of the moon god, Sin, at Harran. Nabonidus objected that this former Assyrian city now lay in the hands of the Medes, who were based in Iran but had occupied the area northwest of Mesopotamia since Assyria's defeat by a coalition of Babylonians and Medes in 612. Marduk, however, promised that the Medes would be no threat to Nabonidus. The god declared that "they and their land and the kings who side with them no longer exist. In the coming third year I shall make Cyrus expel them."

Cyrus the Great, a prince of the Persians, did in fact join a group of disgruntled soldiers to overthrow and supplant his own

On this relief from a stairway in the Persian royal palace at Persepolis, Babylonian dignitaries—whose great imperial city had fallen without resistance to the emperor Cyrus—bring gifts of symbolic tribute to their Persian overlords.

grandfather Astyages, king of the Medes, in 550 BC. This allowed Nabonidus, with whom he may have been allied at the time, access to Harran. Cyrus then became king of both the Medes and the Persians, the first step toward amassing what would become the largest empire the ancient world had ever seen.

But Marduk apparently neglected to warn Nabonidus about Cyrus's eventual control of the Middle East, and the Babylonian ruler, pleased with the success of his Persian counterpart, undertook the rebuilding of the Harran temple to Sin. In this he was doubtless influenced by his priestess mother, Adad-Guppi. A potent figure in her own right, she lived 104 years and was honored after her death with two memorial stones, or steles, offering lengthy accounts of her life and achievements. They were found, in the Harran temple of the moon god, placed near two similar steles commemorating her royal son. One of the stones relates how she too was visited in a dream by the god Sin, urging that her son reconstruct his temple. She goes on to say, "Out of his love for me who worships him and have laid hold to the hem of his garment, Sin, the king of all gods, did what he had not done before, had not granted to anybody else, he gave me [a woman] an exalted position and a famous name in the country."

Meanwhile, Nabonidus's attempts to levy money to rebuild the Harran temple, which had been abandoned for more than 50 years, led to rebellion in Babylon and other cities, whose priests objected to his attempts to increase their taxes and curtail their virtual independence. The king's curious reaction to the crisis, passed down in Babylon's royal chronicles, was to leave his son Belshazzar in command of Babylon and to march into the Arabian desert, where he appears to have spent the next 10 years. Scholars puzzled by Nabonidus's actions have offered several explanations. One asserts that his enemies possibly drove him into exile; another suggests that his sojourn in the desert might actually have been a military foray to patrol and keep open trade routes with Arabia.

While Nabonidus loitered in the desert, events outside the Babylonian empire were sealing its fate. In 10 years of series of military campaigns, Cyrus had amassed, for Persia, lands stretching more than 3,000 miles, from the Aegean Sea to India. Against such a power, Babylon could not hope to survive. According to the Bible, the city's conquest was dramatically predicted during the stewardship of Belshazzar *(page 146)*. While this prince feasted with his guests, a man's hand wrote a frightening message upon the wall of the palace,

Fashioned of alabaster and embellished with bronze, gold, and semiprecious stones, this nearly 10-inch-tall statuette dates from about 250 BC. While the graceful figure reflects the Greek influence of the time, such touches as the bejeweled navel and the gold earrings are survivals from earlier Babylonian days, as is the horned emblem atop her head, an insignia perhaps of her divinity.

"Mene, Mene, Tekel, Upharsin." In Aramaic, Mene means "he counted," Tekel means "he weighed," while Upharsin is the word for "Persian." The message, delivered in this cryptic, oracular manner, clearly needed an interpreter, and after all the court diviners failed to explain it, the line was at last deciphered by the prophet Daniel. Mene, he warned, means, "God hath numbered thy kingdom"; the meaning for Tekel he gave as, "Thou art weighed in the balances and found wanting," and Upharsin was the final blow, "Thy kingdom is divided and given to the Medes and Persians."

The writing was indeed on the wall. A famine and an epidemic of disease afflicting Babylonia were blamed on Nabonidus's desert sojourn; his absence from Babylon, which effectively canceled the New Year's ceremony for many years; and his allegiance to Sin and neglect of Marduk. The king was left with few friends. In 539 BC Cyrus at last turned against his former ally and rapidly overran the country. Then the Persian king marched into Babylon. Nebuchadnezzar's stout walls and canals proved of little use against Cyrus's entry, for it was the internal problems of monarchal mismanagement that ultimately brought the empire down. The population, which saw its kings judged yearly by its gods, welcomed the Persian, a benevolent emperor who seemed favored by heaven. Cleverly, Cyrus had inscribed in a clay cylinder, in cuneiform, the assertion that Marduk himself had ordered him to march against the city and had delivered into his hands "Nabonidus, the king who did not worship him."

Cyrus proved a tolerant ruler of Babylon, maintaining local religious practices and allowing the exiled Jews who wished to do so to return to Jerusalem. Later Persian rulers were not so sympathetic to the city, however: Herodotus tells how in the fifth century BC Cyrus's grandson Xerxes removed the huge gold statue of Marduk from Esagila. Even more destructive for Babylon was the absence of local kings who would have been responsible for maintaining the city's temples, fortifications, and canals. Babylon's buildings inevitably began to decline; Persian immigrants changed the social balance, and the Aramaic language became increasingly strong. Yet against these winds of change, the scribes of the temples held fast, clinging to their traditions, stubbornly retaining cuneiform, and keeping ancient learning alive.

The magnificent city captivated the renowned young Macedonian commander known as Alexander the Great, when in 331 BC he overthrew the Persians and entered the city. He returned seven years later after campaigning across Asia to India, with grandiose plans to make Babylon, along with Alexandria in Egypt, a capital of the world empire he hoped to found. But that ambition would perish with the man, who died suddenly of unknown causes in Babylon in 323 BC at the age of 32.

Babylon would survive a few centuries more, and Mesopotamia would pass along to other civilizations the culmination of its wisdom, accrued over millennia from the time of the Sumerians. Traces of culture from the region between the rivers are detectable not only in the Bible, but also in the myths of ancient Greece, while Hellenistic art and such later religious symbols as the crescent and the Maltese cross drew on the work of Greek sculptors. Some scholars contend that the emphasis on urban life, citizenship, trade, commerce, and literacy, which characterized the Islamic world, was a benefit of the Mesopotamian past, while many Islamic laws resemble their Babylonian and Assyrian forebears. Much of Mesopotamia's legacy may still be unknown, however, with clues awaiting discovery beneath the soil of sites still to be excavated throughout the Middle East.

The Hellenistic occupation of Babylonia was followed by a period of dominance by the Parthians, under whose sway Mesopotamia remained an unconquerable challenge to the power of Rome, the vast new empire in the west. After Jerusalem's destruction by the Romans in AD 70, following a disastrous four-year revolt by its citizens, many of Judaism's rabbis flourished for centuries in Babylonia, where Jewish laws, learning, and oral history were codified into one of two versions—the other written in Palestine—of the comprehensive work known as the Talmud.

But by the end of the second century AD, the city of Babylon was abandoned. The region that had produced pottery, irrigation, the wheel, and writing, as well as the very idea of a city, maintained its impact, for most of its neighbors had become vessels of Mesopotamian culture. After the decline of Rome in the fourth century AD, the Middle East renewed its time-honored stature as the major center, outside the Far East, of literacy and urbanity. It retained this preeminence throughout the European Dark Ages and the Medieval period until the Renaissance, which it helped spawn by preserving many of the great Greek and Roman texts on which that Western revival was based.

REBUILDING BABYLON'S GLORY

Bestriding the thick double walls of ancient Babylon were eight gateways, each named for one of the city's deities. Grandest of all was the gateway dedicated to Ishtar, goddess of love, fertility, and warfare. This great ceremonial entry had been rebuilt three times by Nebuchadnezzar II in the sixth century BC on an ever grander scale.

Glazed in a variety of brilliant colors, Nebuchadnezzar's four-towered Ishtar Gate stood in contrast to the ubiquitous mud brick that made up the rest of the city. Mounted in relief on the gate's blue walls were alternating rows of bulls and dragonlike creatures, symbols of two of Babylon's deities. The bull (*detail above*) depicted the weather god, Adad, while the city's patron god, Marduk, was represented by a remarkable scaly-coated hybrid, with a horned-serpent head, feline front legs, eagle talons on the back legs, and a tail that ended in a scorpion's sting. The gate itself showed no portrayals of the animal associated with Ishtar, the lion.

But on the walled portion of the adjoining Processional Way strode 120 of the mighty beasts in enameled relief, 60 on each side.

Running half a mile from the summer palace to the Ishtar Gate, the Processional Way constituted the main approach route to the most solidly protected city of the ancient world. To successive kings who traveled the lion-lined passage—Nebuchadnezzar, Darius, Xerxes, Alexander—the gateway looming ahead of them must have been a breathtaking sight. The German archaeologists who arrived in Babylon in 1899 and dug down through the rubble of the Ishtar Gate were awed by what they found. Indeed, so captivated were these researchers that they determined to reconstruct the outer gateway as well as the avenue that led up to it, piece by glazed piece. Thirty-one years later, the gateway that had lain deep beneath the dirt and rubble of two millennia stood proudly once more—this time far from home, in Berlin's Vorderasiatisches Museum.

DIGGING DOWN TO BUILD UP

From the beginning of the excavations at Babylon, the archaeologists found everywhere fragments of cracked or broken bricks glazed in bright enamel colors. As they began to uncover the foundations of the Ishtar Gate—which was ornamented with fully preserved bulls and snake-headed beasts in unglazed brick—they realized that many of the enameled pieces they were coming across represented another animal. Only after a year of patiently working with the fragments did the researchers discover that they belonged to the lions that lined the Processional Way.

By the time the First World War put an end to the excavations in 1917, the recovered fragments had been packed into more than 600 cases and stored near the site. Not until 1926 did the British-dominated Iraqi government allow the shipment of the boxes to Germany.

Using a small railway, workers carry dirt away from their excavations of the Ishtar Gate in April 1902. The remains of one of the gate towers—the first excavated part of the structure—display the relief of a bull that was part of the unglazed foundations.

A general view of the excavation site shows how the foundations of the gateway, which went down almost 40 feet, were decorated with bulls and dragons in molded brick. At this northern side of the gate, nine tiers of the animals are visible, amounting to about 150 bulls and dragons in all. The Ishtar Gate was one of Babylon's few surviving well-preserved monuments.

This sectional drawing shows how the Ishtar Gate was really a double gateway, with two portals flanked by four huge towers. The walls of these towers went down so deep—below the level of the water table—that excavators were unable to get to the bottom of them.

PUTTING THE PUZZLE TOGETHER

In Berlin, a team of nine sculptors and molders set about the task of rebuilding Nebuchadnezzar's shattered monument in 1928. The challenge was enormous: Many of the fragments had been found far from their original locations, and to fit a missing piece into place might involve using one recovered 100 yards away from the rest.

The rebuilders systematically sorted the fragments by colors and by body parts of the different animals. Next, they assembled them into bricks, and finally, into complete lions, bulls, and dragons and the various decorative motifs that adorned the structures. Only when they were convinced that a particular brick was indeed missing—many had been reused by locals over the centuries—did they replace it with a modern replica. "We consider ourselves the guardians responsible for a great historical treasure, which we are bound to treat with the greatest care," declared Walter Andrae, the man in charge of the project. "The result will speak for itself and more than repay every effort."

Fragments of glazed brick from the Ishtar Gate and Processional Way are soaked in some of the 200 vats of water that were used to remove the salts that permeated them. Only after a year and a half could the pieces be removed from the vats and preserved with paraffin.

At long worktables, reconstruction workers begin the painstaking job of sorting the hundreds of thousands of pieces of Babylonian glazed brick. "We always get about six to seven fragments for one relief-face of a brick," wrote Andrae, "and the reconstructor must look for two flat bits that fit out of perhaps hundreds of possibilities."

"I laid their foundations at the water table with asphalt and bricks and had them made of bricks with blue stone." So declares Nebuchadnezzar about the walls of the Ishtar Gate in his Great Stone Slab Inscription, seen here reconstructed in modern brick in the Berlin museum. "I placed wild bulls and ferocious dragons in the gateways and thus adorned them with luxurious splendor so that mankind might gaze on them in wonder."

A mason carefully fits together bricks for the reconstruction of the Great Stone Slab inscription. Although archaeologists discovered pieces of the slab lying near the Ishtar Gate, the inscription's original location on the gate is unknown.

SHOWCASING THE FINAL RESULTS

More animals were reconstructed from the brick fragments collected in Babylon than the Berlin museum had room for. In accordance with previous agreements, the Germans delivered completed animals to the Iraq Museum in Baghdad and to Istanbul's Museum of Antiquities. Others were offered to museums in Europe and the United States.

But despite the accuracy with which the animal figures were reassembled, there was little beyond the excavated foundations to guide the rebuilders on the superstructure of the gate. For help they relied on a rectangular gold plate from a Babylonian grave that depicted a great gateway with an arched door, two towers above the walls, and crenelated battlements. The discovery of a number of bricks with more than one glazed face seemed to confirm this design, and the parapet was reconstructed accordingly. The Ishtar Gate and Processional Way were opened to the public in 1930. Surviving World War II, they still stand in a specially built hall of the Vorderasiatisches Museum.

A model on display at the Vorderasiatisches Museum shows how the Ishtar Gate and the walled Processional Way guarded the main entrance to the city of Babylon. It was along this street, known in Babylonian as Aibur-shabu, "the enemy shall never pass," that images of the gods were carried during the New Year Festival.

Snarling lions like this one strode along both sides of the Processional Way, advancing on visitors that approached Babylon from the north. Each of the six-foot-long beasts was made up of 46 bricks laid in 11 rows.

Successive tiers of carved dragons and bulls, symbolizing Babylonian deities, parade around the twin towers of the crenelated Ishtar Gate and through its vaulted corridor in the reconstruction on display in Gallery Nine of the Vorderasiatisches Museum. Although the rebuilt outer gateway has a height of 47 feet, the original is believed to have stood over 75 feet tall.

A SHARED HISTORY BETWEEN THE RIVERS

In the fertile plains between the Tigris and Euphrates, Sumerian civilization began. It was here, around 3500 BC, that cities first appeared, and with them a culture that developed writing, worked in bronze, and used the wheel. As these urban centers grew, they evolved into small city-states linked by trade and a common language and culture. Each city was dominated by the temple of its main god and surrounded by a web of irrigation channels that nourished the parched land.

Water and land were constant sources of conflict among the dozen or so growing city-states of Sumer, however, and much of the third millennium was plagued by chronic warfare. Only when the Akkadian king Sargon the Great forcibly united the whole region under his rule around 2370 BC did the squabbling abate. But Sargon's empire—the world's first—was short-lived. Faced with internal revolt and enemies on its borders, the empire collapsed less than 200 years later. By 2125 BC Ur had asserted itself over the other city-states, and Sumer once again enjoyed a period of revival. Art and literature flourished, and grand building programs were launched.

Around 2000 BC, however, Ur also fell to invaders, and the Sumerian civilization was in decline. But its principal achievements had taken root—literacy, trade, agriculture—and during the centuries to follow Mesopotamian heirs would arise to claim the Sumerian legacy: the mighty Assyrian empire, based in the city of Assur, and Babylon, greatest power of its day.

OLD BABYLONIAN AND OLD ASSYRIAN PERIOD 2000-1600 BC

BRONZE STATUETTE

As Ur's empire crumbled, cities throughout the land grew in prominence, and Mesopotamia splintered into a mosaic of smaller kingdoms. The most important of these cities were Isin and Larsa in the south, and Assur and Mari in the north. Since the end of the third millennium, however, a Semitic people, the Amorites, had been flooding into the region. Quick to absorb the local culture, these immigrants soon rose to positions of power. One monarch of Amorite descent, Shamshi-Adad I, managed to unite Assur and Mari under his rule, creating a northern Mesopotamian empire that established extensive trade links with Anatolia.

In lower Mesopotamia, Amorite rulers built up Babylon to rival Isin and Larsa. Eleven kings made up the ruling First Dynasty of Babylon, but history best remembers the sixth king, Hammurabi, the warrior and lawmaker of the 18th century BC. By diplomacy and successful military campaigns, Hammurabi extended his control over much of Mesopotamia. A succession of lesser rulers followed him, however, and they were unable to take advantage of his rich legacy. By 1721 the empire had shrunk back to the original territory surrounding Babylon. Sometime in the mid 1590s Hittites from Anatolia marched down the Euphrates and captured the city itself.

MIDDLE ASSYRIAN PERIOD 1600-1000 BC

ASSYRIAN ALTAR

The Hittites departed Babylon as quickly as they had come, but their raid marked the beginning of a dark age that lasted several centuries. Peoples who previously played only a minor part in history took advantage of the power vacuum to create new kingdoms. Kassites, whose origins are mysterious, exercised a low-key rule over Babylonia for 400 years. They adopted local customs, religion, and language but were always considered foreigners. Across northern Mesopotamia and Syria, Hurrian-speaking peoples were united into a vast empire called Mitanni. When the Hittites defeated Mitanni in the 14th century, King Ashuruballit of Assyria reasserted his country's independence and paved the way for its ascendancy in the region.

Among the greatest of Assyria's kings in the 13th century was Tukulti-Ninurta I, who captured Babylon. It was the start of an ambivalent relationship between the two Mesopotamian neighbors—of Assyrian military dominance over the south and Babylonian cultural influence in the north. A century later, the reign of Tiglath-Pileser I marked a glorious moment in Assyria's history. This talented and energetic ruler secured the nation's frontiers and extended its influence as far as today's Lebanon. After his death, the western parts of the empire were increasingly harassed by hostile Aramean tribes, however, and Assyria entered a period of uncertainty and decline.

NEO-ASSYRIAN PERIOD 1000-605 BC

STONE RELIEF FROM NINEVEH

Toward the end of the 10th century BC the kingdom on the Tigris was once more on the move. Shaking off its enemies, Assyria regained its lost land, and by the reign of Ashurnasirpal II (883-859 BC) it had reestablished itself as the great power in upper Mesopotamia. A succession of ruthless leaders continued the kingdom's resurgence. They terrorized Assyria's neighbors with policies of conquest, pillage, and mass deportation of defeated peoples, and integrated captured lands into the empire.

With an army trained by years of almost constant fighting, later kings like Sargon II, Sennacherib, and Esarhaddon extended Assyrian hegemony. And during Ashurbanipal's time (668-627 BC) the empire seemed invincible: Babylon had been humbled, Palestine and Syria conquered, and Egypt defeated. But Assyria had overreached itself. Continuous revolts in the provinces had weakened it, and when Chaldean usurpers from the lower Tigris and Euphrates seized the throne of Babylon in 625 BC, the Assyrians were powerless to prevent it. The end came fast. In 614 BC Medes from western Iran sacked Nimrud and Assur, and two years later a coalition of Medes and Babylonian Chaldeans captured Nineveh. In 605 BC Babylon's crown prince Nebuchadnezzar routed the rump of the Assyrian army and its Egyptian allies at Carchemish. The great empire of Assyria was gone, never to revive.

NEO-BABYLONIAN PERIOD 605-539 BC

THE DEMON HUMBABA

During Nebuchadnezzar II's 43-year reign, Babylon underwent a glorious revival. After the fall of Nineveh, the Medes had withdrawn behind the Zagros range to leave the Chaldean rulers of Babylon as sole masters of Mesopotamia. Nebuchadnezzar seized Assyria's former provinces of Syria and Palestine, sacked Jerusalem and carried off the Jews into captivity, and launched a colossal building program in the south of the country. His capital city of Babylon, enlarged and rebuilt, became the center of an architectural and scientific renaissance, and a Chaldean empire replaced that of Assyria.

The Babylonian renewal was brilliant but brief, like the empire of Hammurabi before it. After Nebuchadnezzar's death in 562 BC, there followed a twilight period, presided over by ineffectual rulers incapable of resisting the new threat from the east. The Persians had already defeated their neighbors, the Medes, and when they dispatched an army toward Babylonia, the writing was on the wall. In 539 BC the Persian king, Cyrus the Great, arrived at the gates of the most magnificent walled city the world had ever seen. After a brief struggle, he and his army entered Babylon, which would never again be an independent kingdom.

PERSIAN AND HELLENISTIC PERIOD 539-126 BC

PERSIAN DRINKING HORN

Unlike other foreign rulers, the Persians did not come to Babylon just to set up a new dynasty. Although Cyrus showed respect for local traditions, other forces were at work in the Middle East. Babylonia and the still-ruined land of Assyria took their place as the ninth satrapy, or jurisdiction, of the Persian empire, and Babylon survived only as a minor provincial capital.

Babylon's prospects revived with the arrival of Alexander the Great, who captured the city from the retreating Persians in 331 BC. Hailed as liberator by the Babylonians, the Macedonian king pushed on to the east, as far as the Ganges River, before returning to the city he planned to make his eastern capital. Babylon, it seemed, was about to regain its former greatness. But when Alexander died there in 323 BC of a fever, the city's hopes were dashed.

After suffering under Alexander's squabbling generals, Babylon and the Asian provinces eventually passed to Seleucus, chief of the Macedonian cavalry. His descendants, the Seleucids, began building new cities, and Greek became the common tongue of the land. Nebuchadnezzar's once mighty city gradually lost its importance, and Babylon finally succumbed to one last invader, the dust and sand of the encroaching deserts.

ACKNOWLEDGMENTS

The editors thank these individuals and institutions for their valuable assistance in the preparation of this volume:

Ernest Walter Andrae, Bad Lieben-zell; Rainer Michael Boehmer, Deutsches Archäologisches Institut, Berlin; John A. Brinkman, Oriental Institute, Chicago; Dominique Collon, British Museum, London; Elizabeth Fontan, Conservateur en Chef Département des Antiquités, Musée du Louvre, Paris; Brigitte Gaspar, Staatliche Museen zu Berlin-Preussischer Kulturbesitz, Vorderasiatisches Museum, Berlin; A. Invernizzi, Cen-tro Ricerche Archeologiche e Scavi, Turin; Heidrun Klein, Bildarchiv Preussischer Kulturbesitz, Berlin; Evelyn Klengel-Brandt, Staatliche Museen zu Berlin-Preussischer Kulturbesitz, Vorderasiatisches Museum, Berlin; Kai Kohlmeyer, Staatliche Museen zu Berlin-Preussischer Kulturbesitz Museum für Vor-und Frühgeschichte, Berlin; Jean-Claude Margueron, Paris; Joachim Marzahn, Staatliche Museen zu Berlin-Preussischer Kulturbesitz, Vorderasiatisches Museum, Berlin; Hans Nissen, Seminar für Vorderasia-tische Altertumskunde, Freie Univer-sität, Berlin; Joan Oates, Cambridge, England; Françoise Quersonnier, Lafarge-Coppée, Paris; Julian Reade, British Museum, London; Denise Schmandt-Besserat, Austin, Texas; Hansjörg Schmid, Freie Universität, Berlin; Henry Carter Shaffer, Boston College, Massachusetts; David Stronach, University of California, Berkeley; Geneviève Teissier, Départe-ment des Antiquités Orientales, Musée du Louvre, Paris; Steve Tinney, University of Pennsylvania, Philadel-phia; David Ussishkin, Tel Aviv Uni-versity, Tel Aviv.

PICTURE CREDITS

The Age of God-Kings: TimeFrame 3000-1500 BC (TimeFrame series). Alexandria, Va.: Time-Life Books, 1987.

Albright, William Foxwell. *The Biblical Period from Abraham to Ezra.* New York: Harper & Row, 1963.

Amiet, Pierre. *Art of the Ancient Near East.* Translated by John Shepley and Claude Choquet. New York: Harry N. Abrams, 1980.

Andrae, E. W., and R. M. Boehmer. *Sketches by an Excavator.* Berlin: Gebr. Mann Verlag, 1992.

Barbarian Tides: TimeFrame 1500-600 BC (TimeFrame series). Alexandria, Va.: Time-Life Books, 1987.

Black, Jeremy, and Anthony Green. *Gods, Demons and Symbols of Ancient Mesopotamia.* Austin: University of Texas Press, 1992.

Campbell, Joseph. *The Mythic Image.* Princeton: Princeton University Press, 1974.

Caygill, Marjorie. *Treasures of the British Museum.* New York: Harry N. Abrams, 1985.

Ceram, C. W. (ed.). *Hands on the Past: Pioneer Archaeologists Tell Their Own Story.* New York: Alfred A. Knopf, 1966.

Chiera, Edward. *They Wrote on Clay: The Babylonian Tablets Speak Today.* Chicago: University of Chicago Press, 1966.

Clayton, Peter A., and Martin J. Price. *The Seven Wonders of the Ancient World.* London: Routledge, 1988.

Collon, Dominique:
First Impressions: Cylinder Seals in the Ancient Near East. Chicago: University of Chicago Press, 1987.
Interpreting the Past. London: British Museum Publications, 1990.

Contenau, Georges. *Everyday Life in Babylon and Assyria.* London: Edward Arnold, 1954.

Crawford, Vaughn E., Prudence O. Harper, and Holly Pittman. *Assyrian Reliefs and Ivories in the Metropolitan Museum of Art: Palace Reliefs of Ashurnasirpal II and Ivory Carvings from Nimrud.* New York: The Metropolitan Museum of Art, 1980.

Curtis, John (ed.). *Fifty Years of Mesopotamian Discovery: The Work of the British School of Archaeology in Iraq, 1932-1982.* London: The British School of Archaeology in Iraq , 1982.

Davidson, Marshall B. (ed.). *The Horizon Book of Lost Worlds.* New York: American Heritage, 1962.

Deuel, Leo (ed.). *The Treasures of Time.* London: Souvenir Press, 1962.

Fagan, Brian M. *Return to Babylon.* Boston: Little Brown, 1979.

Farkas, Ann E., Prudence O. Harper, and Evelyn B. Harrison (eds). *Monsters and Demons in the Ancient and Medieval Worlds.* Mainz: Philipp von Zabern, 1987.

Finegan, Jack. *Archaeological History of the Ancient Middle East.* New York: Dorset Press, 1979.

Finkel, Irving L. "The Hanging Gardens of Babylon." In *The Seven Wonders of the Ancient World,* edited by Peter A. Clayton and Martin J. Price. New York: Dorset Press, 1989.

Frankfort, Henri. *The Art and Architecture of the Ancient Orient.* London: Penguin Books, 1970.

Freedman, David Noel (ed.). *The Anchor Bible Dictionary* (Vol. 1). New York: Doubleday, 1992.

Gray, John. *Near Eastern Mythology.* New York: Peter Bedrick, 1985.

Hackett, John (ed.). *Warfare in the Ancient World.* New York: Facts on File, 1990.

Hawkes, Jacquetta (ed.). *The World of the Past.* New York: Alfred A. Knopf, 1963.

The Holy Land (Lost Civilizations series). Alexandria, Va.: Time-Life Books, 1992.

Jacobsen, Thorkild. *The Harps That Once . . .: Sumerian Poetry in Translation.* New Haven: Yale University Press, 1987.

Jakob-Rost, Liane, et. al. *The Museum of the Near East* (National Museum of Berlin). Mainz: Philipp von Zabern, 1992.

Keller, Werner. *The Bible As History.* Translated by William Neil. New York: William Morrow, 1981.

Klengel-Brandt, Evelyn. *Der Turm von Babylon: Legende Und Geschichte Eines Bauwerkes.* Berlin: Koehler & Amelang, 1982.

Koldewey, Robert. *The Excavations at Babylon.* Translated by Agnes S. Johns. London: Macmillan, 1914.

Kramer, Samuel Noah, and the Editors of Time-Life Books. *Cradle of Civilization* (Great Ages of Man series). New York: Time Incorporated, 1967.

Larsen, Mogens Trolle (ed.). *Mesopotamia: Copenhagen Studies in Assyriology* (Vol. 7). Copenhagen: Akademisk Forlag, 1979.

Lee, Sidney (ed.). *Dictionary of National Biography* (Vol. 48). London: Smith, Elder, 1896.

Lloyd, Seton:
The Archaeology of Mesopotamia. London: Thames and Hudson, 1978.
Foundations in the Dust: The Story of Mesopotamian Exploration. London: Thames and Hudson, 1980.

McCall, Henrietta. *Mesopotamian Myths.* Austin: University of Texas Press and British Museum Publications, 1990.

McKenzie, John L., *Dictionary of the Bible.* Milwaukee: The Bruce Publishing Co., 1965.

Magnusson, Magnus. *BC: The Archaeology of the Bible Lands.* London: Bodley Head and British Broadcasting Corp., 1977.

Mallowan, Max. *Mallowan's Memoirs.* London: Collins, 1977.

Marzahn, Joachim. *The Ishtar Gate: The Processional Way/The New Year Festival of Babylon.* Translated by Biri Fay and Robert K. Englund. Mainz: Philipp von Zabern, 1992.

Merhav, Rivka (ed.). *Treasures of the Bible Lands: The Elie Borowski Collection.* Tel Aviv: Tel Aviv Museum and Modan Publishers, 1987.

Millard, Alan. *Treasures from Bible Times.* Tring, Hertfordshire, England: Lion Publishing, 1985.

Moorey, P. R. S.:
Ancient Iraq. Oxford: The Ashmolean Museum, 1976.
Ur 'of the Chaldees'. Ithaca, N.Y.: Cornell University Press, 1982.

Moortgat, Anton. *The Art of Ancient Mesopotamia: The Classical Art of the Near East.* London: Phaidon, 1969.

Muscarella, Oscar White (ed.). *Ladders to Heaven: Art Treasures from Lands of the Bible.* Toronto: McClelland and Stewart, 1981.

Nissen, Hans J., Peter Damerow, and Robert K. Englund. *Archaic Bookkeeping.* Translated by Paul Larsen. Chicago: University of Chicago Press, 1993.

Oates, Joan. *Babylon.* London: Thames and Hudson, 1986.

O'Neill, John P. (ed.). *Egypt and the*

Ancient Near East. New York: The Metropolitan Museum of Art, 1987.

Oppenheim, A. Leo. *Ancient Mesopotamia: Portrait of a Dead Civilization.* Chicago: University of Chicago Press, 1977.

Oppenheim, A. Leo (transl.). *Letters From Mesopotamia.* Chicago: University of Chicago Press, 1967.

Parrot, André:
The Arts of Assyria. Translated by Stuart Gilbert and James Emmons. New York: Golden Press, 1961.
Babylon and the Old Testament. Translated by B. E. Hooke. London: SCM Press, 1958.
Discovering Buried Worlds. New York: Philosophical Library, 1955.
Mari. Munich: Hanns Reich Verlag, 1953.
Nineveh and the Old Testament. New York: Philosophical Library, 1955.
The Tower of Babel. Translated by Edwin Hudson. London: SCM Press, 1955.
Ziggurats et Tour de Babel. Paris: Éditions Albin Michel, 1949.

Postgate, J. N. *Early Mesopotamia: Society and Economy at the Dawn of History.* London: Routledge, 1992.

Postgate, Nicholas. *The First Empires.* Oxford: Elsevier Phaidon, 1977.

Pritchard, James B. *The Ancient Near East in Pictures Relating to the Old Testament.* Princeton: Princeton University Press, 1954.

Pritchard, James B. (ed.):
The Ancient Near East: An Anthology of Texts and Pictures (Vols. 1 and 2). Princeton: Princeton University Press, 1973.
Ancient Near Eastern Texts Relating to the Old Testament. Princeton: Princeton University Press, 1969.
The Harper Atlas of the Bible. New York: Harper & Row, 1987.

Quarantelli, Ezio (ed.). *The Land between Two Rivers.* Translated by Juliet Haydock and Michael Binns. Turin: Il Quadrante Edizioni, 1985.

Reade, Julian. *Assyrian Sculpture.* Cambridge: Harvard University Press, 1983.

Roaf, Michael. *Mesopotamia and the Ancient Near East.* Alexandria, Va.: Stonehenge Press, 1990.

Roux, Georges. *Ancient Iraq.* London: Penguin Books, 1992.

Russell, John Malcolm. *Sennacherib's Palace without Rival at Nineveh.* Chicago: University of Chicago Press, 1992.

Saggs, H. W. F.:
Civilization before Greece and Rome. New Haven: Yale University Press, 1989.
Everyday Life in Babylonia & Assyria. New York: G. P. Putnam's, 1965.
The Greatness That Was Babylon: A Survey of the Ancient Civilization of the Tigris-Euphrates Valley. New York: Hawthorn, 1962.
The Might That Was Assyria. New York: St. Martin's Press, 1984.

Scarre, Chris. *Smithsonian Timelines of the Ancient World.* London: Dorling-Kindersley, 1993.

Schmandt-Besserat, Denise. *Before Writing: From Counting to Cuneiform* (Vol. 1). Austin: University of Texas Press, 1992.

Sievernich, Gereon, and Hendrik Budde. *Europe and the Orient, 800-1900.* Munich: Bertelsmann Lexicon Verlag, 1989.

Speiser, E. A. (transl.). *The Anchor Bible: Genesis.* Garden City: Doubleday, 1982.

Stone, Elizabeth. "Urban Density and Layout." In *The Ancient Near East,* edited by J. Sasson. New York: Scribners, in press.

Strommenger, Eva. *5000 Years of the Art of Mesopotamia.* New York: Harry N. Abrams, 1964.

Sumer: Cities of Eden (Lost Civilizations series). Alexandria, Va.: Time-Life Books, 1993.

Unger, Eckhard. *Babylon: Die Heilige Stadt Nach der Beschreibung der Babylonier.* Berlin: Walter de Gruyter, 1931.

Ussishkin, David. *The Conquest of Lachish by Sennacherib.* Tel Aviv: Tel Aviv University, 1982.

Von Soden, Wolfram. *The Ancient Orient: An Introduction to the Study of the Ancient Near East.* Translated by Donald G. Schley. Grand Rapids: William B. Eerdmans, 1994.

Walker, C. B. F. *Reading the Past: Cuneiform.* Berkeley: University of California Press, 1987.

Waterfield, Gordon. *Layard of Nineveh.* New York: Frederick A. Praeger, 1963.

Weiss, Harvey (ed.). *Ebla to Damascus: Art and Archaeology of Ancient Syria.* Washington, D.C.: Smithsonian Institution, 1985.

Wilhelm, Gernot. *The Hurrians.* Translated by Jennifer Barnes. Warminster, England: Aris and Phillips, 1989.

Winstone, H. V. F.:
Uncovering the Ancient World. New York: Facts on File, 1985.
Woolley of Ur: The Life of Sir Leonard Woolley. London: Secker and Warburg, 1990.

Zettler, Richard L. *Nippur III: Kassite Buildings in Area WC-1* (Vol. 3). Chicago: The Oriental Institute of The University of Chicago, 1993.

PERIODICALS:

Armstrong, James A. "West of Edin: Tell al-Deylam and the Babylonian City of Dilbat." *Biblical Archaeologist,* December 1992.

"BARlines." *Biblical Archaeology Review,* July/August 1993.

Biblical Archaeology Review, March/April 1984.

British Museum Magazine, Winter 1993.

Collon, Dominique. "Les Trésors de Nimroud." *Le Monde de la Bible,* July/August 1991.

Damerji, Muayad Said. "The Second Treasure of Nimrud." *Near Eastern Studies,* 1991.

Elmer-DeWitt, Philip. "The Golden Treasures of Nimrud." *Time,* October 30, 1989.

Expedition, Summer 1981.

Gorelick, Leonard, and A. John Gwinnett:
"The Ancient Near Eastern Cylinder Seal as Social Emblem and Status Symbol." *Journal of Near Eastern Studies,* January 1990.
"Close Work without Magnifying Lenses?" *Expedition,* Winter 1981.
"The Origin and Development of the Ancient Near Eastern Cylinder Seal: A Hypothetical Reconstruction." *Expedition,* Summer 1981.

Gwinnett, A. John, and Leonard Gorelick. "The Change from Stone Drills to Copper Drills in Mesopotamia." *Expedition,* Vol. 29, No. 3, 1987.

Moorey, P. R. S. "The Terracotta Plaques from Kish and Hursagkalama, c. 1850 to 1650 B.C." *Iraq,* Vol. 37, Autumn 1975.

Ozguc, Tabsin. "An Assyrian Trading

Outpost." *Scientific American*, February 1963.

Schmandt-Besserat, Denise. "The Origins of Writing: An Archaeologist's Perspective." *Written Communication*, Vol. 3, No. 1, January 1986.

Stone, Elizabeth C. "Chariots of the Gods in Old Babylonian Mesopotamia (c. 2000-1600 BC)." *Cambridge Archaeological Journal*, March 1, 1993.

Stone, Elizabeth C., and Paul Zimansky. "Mashkan-shapir and the Anatomy of an Old Babylonian City." *Biblical Archaeologist*, December 1992.

Stronach, David, and Stephen Lumsden. "UC Berkeley's Excavations at Nineveh." *Biblical Archaeologist*, December 1992.

Weiss, H., et. al. "The Genesis and Collapse of Third Millennium North Mesopotamian Civilization." *Science*, August 20, 1993.

Weiss, Harvey. "On the Habur Plains of Syria." *Biblical Archaeologist*, March 1985.

Wilford, John Noble. "Ancient Clay Horse Is Found in Syria." *New York Times*, January 3, 1993.

OTHER:

Armstrong, James A., and Margaret Catlin Brandt, "Ancient Dunes at Nippur." Study (draft), 1994.

Kohlmeyer, Kay, Eva Strommenger, and Hansjörg Schmid. *Babylon Rearisen*. Accompaniment text for the exhibition "Babylon Rearisen," presented by the National Museum of Prussian Culture. Berlin: Enka Druck, 1991.

Syrie: Mémoire et Civilisation. Catalog. Nantes: Institut du Monde Arabe Exposition, September 14, 1993 to April 30, 1994.

The Westminster Theological Journal, No. 39. Philadelphia: Fall 1977.

Lamashtu (demon): 69, 142
Lamgi-Mari: statuette of, 8, 11
Larsa: 19, 20, 21, 22, 27, 29, 35, 36, 158
Law: Assyrian legal codes, 62, 66-67; code of Eshnunna, 28; Code of Hammurabi, 26-29; code of Ur-Nammu, 28; court documents, 30-32; Islamic codes, 150; Mosaic code, 28
Layard, Henry Austen: 86, 94, 107, 111, 112, 115; excavations by, 68, 88-89, 90-93, 94, 114; publication of *Nineveh and Its Remains*, 91; transport of Assyrian bull colossi to British Museum, *116-117*
Literature: epic poetry, 60-61
Louvre: 26, 87, 112, 118, 119; Assyrian bull colossi at, *120, 121*

M

McCown, Donald: 30
Mallowan, Max: 111; excavations at Nimrud, 93-95, 100
Mamelukes: 124
Marduk (deity): 21, 22, 26, 45, 60, 111, 130, *131*, 139, 147, 149, 151; bronze symbol of, *122*
Marduk-Zakir-Shumi: *105*
Mari: 20, 21, 29, 52, 54, 158; excavations at, 7-8, *10*, 11-14; tablets found at, 14-16, 53
Mashkan-shapir: 21, 29; abandonment of, 34; canals in, 32-33; excavations at, 32-33
Mathematics: Babylonian achievements in, 16, 143-144; cuneiform tablets on, *16*
Medes: 110, 147, 148, 159
Medicine: Assyrian practices, 68-69; Babylonian advances in, 144
Mediterranean Sea: 9, 97, 105
Megiddo: 57
Memphis: 109
Mesopotamia: archaeological rivalry of Britain and France in, 87-88, 90; archival tablets and details of daily life, 14-16; chariot and horse in, 33-34, *103*; cultural legacy of, 150; diplomatic activity in, 56, 58-59; economic and ecological crises in, 34-37; geographic divisions in, 8; identification of chronological periods, 9; irrigation in, 17, 34-35, 38, 140, 158; search for antiquities, 9-11; social stratification in, 27; species depletion in, 70; struggle for domination in, 7, 9, 17; and Sumer, 16-17, 158; trade in,

32, 48, 50, 144; urban life in, 8-9, 158; widespread unrest and displacement in, 61
Middle Assyrian period: 9, 48-50, 57, 158; re-creation of life in, 62-67
Mitanni: 55-57, 58, 59, 69, 158
Mohammad Keritli Oglu: 86-87, 89-90
Moses: 28
Mosul: 85, 88, 89, 93
Mount Lebanon: 97
Mulisu: tomb of, 80
Museum of Antiquities (Istanbul): 156
Mushku: 69
Muzahim Mahmoud Hussein: 111; excavations at Nimrud, 79-80, 81, 95

N

Nabonidus: *145*-149
Nabopolassar: 39, 131, 134
Nabu (deity): 63, 95
Nabu Temple (Nimrud): 95
Nebuchadnezzar II: 7, 29, 39, 124, 133, 134, 144, 146, 159; conquest of Jerusalem, 138; death of, 145; and Hanging Gardens of Babylon, 135-136; and Ishtar Gate, 151, 154, 155; rebuilding of Babylon, 130-131; throne room of, 134-135, *137*
Necho: 111
Neo-Assyrian period: 9, 50, 70, 81, 159
Neo-Babylonian period: 9, 124, 159
Nergal (deity): 33
Nimrod: 41
Nimrud: 85, 86, 93, 112, 159; excavations at, 79-81, 82, 88-89, 94-95; founding of, 96; gold artifacts found at, *82-84*; ivory found at, 94-95, *98-99*; Northwest Palace at, 86, 94, 100, 116; Shalmaneser's palace, 100-101; throne room of Ashurnasirpal II, *90*; tombs at, 79-81, 82; Treasury, *106-107*
Nineveh: 9, 22, 26, 52, 56, 62, 69, 86, 88, 101, 112; Ashurbanipal's library at, 60, 68, 92, 110; excavations at, 91-93, 108-109, 110-111; fall of, 110-111, 131, 159; inscriptions found at, 107; palace reliefs found at, *71-77, 108-109*; Sennacherib's palace at, 92, 108-109, 114
Nineveh and Its Remains, 91
Ninkarrak (deity): 133
Ninurta (deity): 32
Nippur: 29; abandonment of, 36-37; clay map of, *34*; excavations at, 30, 35; tablets found at, 28

Nuzi: tablets found at, 56-57, 62; terra cotta found at, *58*

O

Oates, David: excavations at Nimrud, 101; excavations at Tell al-Rimah, 53
Oates, Joan: 94
Obelisks: 91, *95*
Old Babylonian and Old Assyrian period: 9, 48, 141, 158
Opis: 20
Oriental Institute (University of Chicago): 30, 118
Orontes River: 97, 102

P

Parrot, André: excavations at Tell Hariri (Mari), 7-8, 11-14, 20, 53
Parthians: 150
Pazuzu (deity): *142*
Persepolis: reliefs at, *147*
Persian Gulf: 9
Persians: drinking horn, *159*; rise to empire, 147-149, 159
Phoenicians: 98, 144
Place, Victor: 89, 112, 118, 120
Pythagoras: 144

R

Ramses II: 59
Ramses III: 61
Rassam, Hormuzd: 93
Rawlinson, Henry: 88, 93
Reade, Julian: 86
Religion: Assyrian altar, *63, 158;* Assyrian rituals, 67-68; Babylonian New Year's festival, 130, 138-139, 145, 149, 156; Babylonian rituals, 138-139; divination, 68-69, *96-97,* 142, 143; divination tablet, *17;* patron deities, 158; quests for authenticity of biblical accounts, 31; shamanism, 69; Talmud, 150; temple bureaucracy, 139-141
Rembrandt: painting by, *146*
Rich, Claudius James: explorations in ruins of Babylon, 123-124, 125-126
Rich, Mary: 123
Rim-Sin: 20-21
Rossini, Gioacchino Antonio: 102
Royal Asiatic Society: 93
Royal Museums (Berlin): 127